M000218071

THE EYES HAVE IT

THE EYES HAVE IT

Revealing Their Power, Messages, and Secrets

Evan Marshall

CITADEL PRESS
Kensington Publishing Corp.
www.kensingtonbooks.com

Grateful acknowledgment is made for permission to use an ex-
cerpt from the article "Attitude and Pupil Size" by Eckhard H.
Hess, *Scientific American,* April 1965.

All photographs © Corbis.

CITADEL PRESS BOOKS are published by

Kensington Publishing Corp.
850 Third Avenue
New York, NY 10022

All Kensington titles, imprints, and distributed lines are available
at special quantity discounts for bulk purchases for sales promo-
tions, premiums, fund-raising, educational, or institutional use.
Special book excerpts or customized printings can also be created
to fit specific needs. For details, write or phone the office of the
Kensington special sales manager: Kensington Publishing Corp.,
850 Third Avenue, New York, NY 10022, attn: Special Sales
Department, phone: 1-800-221-2647.

First Kensington printing: February 2003
10 9 8 7 6 5 4 3 2 1

Printed in the United States of America

Cataloging data may be obtained from the Library of Congress.

ISBN 0-8065-2445-6

The eyes of men converse as much as their tongues, with the advantage that the occular dialect needs no dictionary, but is understood the world over.

—Ralph Waldo Emerson

CONTENTS

Introduction   1

1. TO LOOK, OR NOT TO LOOK
   Speaking the Language of the Eyes   9

2. THE PHYSICAL EYE
   A Guide to Physiognomy   33

3. DRINK TO ME ONLY . . .
   The Eye Language of Love   69

4. SILENT INTRUSION
   The Etiquette of Staring   87

5. THE VITAL BLINK
   Eye Cut-Offs   101

6. THE EVIL EYE—PAST AND PRESENT
   Eye-Domination Through the Ages   115

7. SECRETS OF THE INNER EYE
   Pupillometry and Iridology   139

8. EYE ADORNMENT
   The Language of Beauty   157

Index   169

THE EYES HAVE IT

INTRODUCTION

Opening the Windows of the Soul

During the 1970s, '80s, and '90s, those decades of frantic self-exploration, a number of books appeared on the subject of human behavior and nonverbal communication, or "body language." As caught up in this movement as anyone, I read these volumes avidly, and noticed that nearly every one cited eye behavior as one of the subtlest of all forms of nonverbal communication.

I have always been intrigued by the eyes as symbols of beauty and mystery. Reading these books, I became fascinated by their communicative powers, and began searching for a book devoted solely to the many aspects of "eye language." I found one or two scholarly works that addressed patterns of eye contact and the direction of gaze, but these were highly technical, having been written primarily for psychologists, and they were limited in scope.

I continued to search, and although I could find no one popular work on all the aspects of eye language,

I did discover more than enough scattered material, not to mention the researchers who had generated it, to warrant the writing of such a book. With great excitement, I undertook this task.

One of my first findings was that the notion of a link between emotions and eye behavior was not new, but could be traced all the way back to the 1870s. In 1872, thirteen years after the publication of his earth-shaking *The Origin of the Species,* Charles Darwin wrote *The Expression of the Emotions in Man and Animals.* His primary question in writing this book was whether our basic facial expressions originated in primitive, functional acts still performed by the creatures of the animal kingdom, and "whether the same expression and gestures prevail . . . with all races of mankind"; in other words, are they universal? To find out, he sent a questionnaire to correspondents throughout the world, asking such questions as: "Is astonishment expressed by the eyes and mouth being opened wide, and the eyebrows being raised?" "When considering deeply on any subject, or trying to understand any puzzle, does he frown, or wrinkle the skin beneath the lower eyelids?"

Though Darwin's book raised a number of interesting possibilities, it hadn't nearly the effect of his other book, for it was not until 1946 that an anthropologist named Ray Birdwhistell took up the study of body motion and even coined a name for this study: kinesics.

Birdwhistell's investigations began when, while living among the Kutenai Indians of western Canada as part of a research project, he noticed that the Indians looked different—their smiles, nods, and general body movements changed—when speaking English than they did when speaking Kutenai. He went on to study body-movement differences between people of various nationalities, and in 1959 set up a laboratory for this purpose at Philadelphia's Eastern Pennsylvania Psychiatric Institute. Later, as Senior Research Scientist and Director of the Studies in Human Communication Project, he continued his work in kinesics, using as his "manual" a catalogue of individual body movements that he called kines (the least perceptible) and kinemes (the larger and more significant). Americans, he found, use between fifty and sixty basic kinemes, thirty-three of which are of the face and head. These latter include four eyebrow positions (lifted, lowered, knit, and single-brow movement) and four eyelid positions. Just as a word's meaning may change according to the context in which it is used, a kineme is a unit whose meaning may depend upon the other kinemes and the words that accompany it. In addition to his kineme catalogue, Birdswhistell even devised an ingenious notation system of symbols for recording subjects' kinemes: an almond shape for an open eye, a horizontal line for a closed eye, and so on.

Over the years, Birdwhistell confirmed a number of observations about kines and kinemes. Some, for example, are virtually inseparable from speech—a slight lowering of the eyelids at the end of a sentence, a widening of the eyes at the end of a question. Others may contradict spoken language. When this happens, it is usually the kines or kinemes that speak the truth. Two eye-language examples are the person who professes his undying affection while his eyes reveal pure indifference, or conversely, the person whose voice is flat and emotionless while his eyes betray the fullness of his heart.

Psychologist Silvan Tomkins agreed with Birdwhistell that the face is a key site of emotion, but also sought the reason why. In his two-volume work, *Affect, Imagery, Consciousness,* he writes that when we feel an emotion, the brain sends messages to the face that cause the contraction and relaxation of certain muscles. Tomkins even theorizes that the feeling we get from the way these muscles contract and relax is a subconscious cue to what basic emotions we're feeling. For each of these facially displayed emotions, or "affects"— interest/excitement, enjoyment/joy, surprise/startle, distress/anguish, shame/humiliation, contempt/disgust, anger/rage, and fear/terror—there are one or more unique configurations in what Tomkins defines as the three main areas of the face: the mouth, the brows, and the eyes. Note that two of these areas consist of the eyes and the skin around them.

Paul Ekman, one of the leading psychologists in the field of nonverbal communication, took the study of facial expressions a step further. In collaboration with Wallace Friesen and Silvan Tomkins, he created a system of decoding these expressions—Facial Affect Scoring Technique, or FAST. Much as a police artist combines various eyes, noses, and mouths to re-create the face of a suspect, FAST uses photographs of "partials" in three areas of the face (forehead and brows;

eyes; nose, cheeks, mouth, chin) to simulate complex facial expressions.

Using FAST, Ekman trained students to correctly interpret the emotions displayed by people's expressions. These students begin with the basic emotions, then proceed to blends (seemingly contradictory combinations), easily confused signals (such as those for "surprise" and "hurt"), and the recognition of honest versus dishonest, or feigned, signals.

As we've established, most of our facial signals occur in the area of the eyes, and each signal may possess a number of subtly varying meanings, depending upon the context (language, accompanying signals) in which it is used. Even without special training, instinctively we all know the meanings of many of these signals. Blinking, for example, may indicate either surprise or attention, winking, confidentiality, or flirtation. Widened eyes may signal amazement or appetite, while closed eyes may be a sign of anything from sorrow to simple concentration. Consider the range of possible meanings in a stare: a dull gaze of apathy or boredom; a brightly transfixed look of fascination or wonder; a clouded gaze of incomprehension or disbelief; cold eyes of aggression; bold eyes of sexual attraction. Eyes that shift sideways may signal deception or doubt; lowered eyes may indicate guilt, embarrassment, modesty, or obedience. And a gesture as simple as lowering the eyelids has proven as powerful as any lover's magic.

There are even signals involving only the eyebrows. Raising them may convey greeting, flirtation, or inquisitiveness; raising only one may express skepticism or ask a question of a very personal nature. Lowering the eyebrows may show disapproval or confusion. Even the eyebrow wiggle has a meaning—it's an unmistakable gesture of sexual suggestion.

Add to this "ocular dictionary" the many gestures that involve both the eyes and the hands—from the eye-point to the eye-rub to the eyelid-pull (not to mention the gestures we perform with accessories such as eyeglasses)—and the eyes could be said to speak a language as richly versatile and subtly complex as any spoken language. The difference is that words are almost always consciously chosen, and therefore can—and often do—express insincere or intentionally deceitful sentiments. Body mannerisms—including the most subtle mannerisms of the eyes—can also be faked, but more often they are instinctive or unconscious, indicators of our *true* thoughts and motivations.

Consider a day in the life of your eyes. With that first look in the bathroom mirror they're giving you a status report on your physical condition. Are they bloodshot? Puffy? Dark-circled? The people you encounter today will gather small impressions from these physical clues, and if you alter your eyes' appearance in any way—makeup, eyeglasses, sunglasses—you're making a silent but strong statement about how you want to be perceived.

You'll elaborate on this statement through your patterns of looking and not looking—at co-workers, friends, family members. Tonight, if it's your night for romance, you can rely on your eyes to speak of love more eloquently than words ever could, whether by holding the gaze of that attractive stranger at the other end of the bar, or by gazing on your lover with irises dilated by the truest affection. And when at last your eyes close for sleep—the ultimate "cut-off"—they're providing your brain with a vital rest that will allow you to awaken fresh for the new day.

Very rarely do we say what—or all—we're really thinking, so it's natural that we investigate every possible means of getting beneath the surface, of learning to be aware of and to understand languages more expressive and reliable than the spoken one. Of these other languages, that of the eyes speaks most revealingly of all. No other of our features, physical or spiritual, says so much about us, in so many different ways. Through the ages we've known this instinctively, and have instilled no other object with as much religious, sexual, and psychological significance as the human eye.

Some equate a person's eyes with his identity. Censoring black bars placed over the eyes of people in photographs assure virtual anonymity, as do the eye-covering masks and cowls worn by our favorite super-heroes (Batman, for example) and outlaws (Zorro) to conceal their alter identities, as well as the elegantly brief masks worn at the masquerade balls of another age.

Carved by early man into the walls of caves, worshipped as gods by the greatest civilizations, celebrated for their romantic properties—as "windows of the soul"—by poets and painters alike, the eyes, according to Ralph Waldo Emerson, are "bold as lions—roving, running, leaping . . . what inundation of life and thought is discharged from one soul into another through them!"

The eyes are the key to unlocking the secrets of our innermost thoughts, to gaining insights into ourselves and others that will enrich our lives in love, health, career. Best of all, they are before us for the reading, in every person we will ever encounter over the course of our lives.

This book is your guide to this fascinating silent language. When you are finished, you will be able to put this powerful means of communication to use, speaking and understanding the signals we are constantly sending one another with our eyes.

1

TO LOOK, OR NOT TO LOOK

Speaking the Language of the Eyes

For eyes can speak and eyes can understand.

—George Chapman, *The Gentleman Usher*

When the eyes say one thing, and the tongue another, a practiced man relies on the language of the first.

—Ralph Waldo Emerson, *The Conduct of Life*

The Grammar of the Eyes

"What is your book about?" my friend asked, her eyes fixed brightly on mine.

"Eye language," I replied.

Her gaze wandered as she thought for a moment; then she looked back at me. "Oh, you mean, how we speak with our eyes?"

When I nodded, her eyes darted away, and they refused to meet mine more than two fleeting times for the rest of the conversation.

I could have predicted her reaction, for this exchange had taken place many times before. Like someone who refuses to have his palm read because he fears the prediction, my friends quickly withdrew their eyes from the danger of being "read." To their minds, I knew something about them that even they did not know. Whatever it was I might read in their eyes, they weren't about to let me try.

Ironically, what my friends may not have realized is that this sort of gaze aversion is as telling as a steady stare. In fact, it is the pattern of looking *and* not looking that acts as an important channel of nonverbal communication in virtually all face-to-face encounters.

In every culture there is a basic pattern of conversational eye behavior that is neither arbitrary nor accidental, but follows definite rules. Our eyes convey silent messages, express our personalities, and keep our conversations running smoothly by adding a silent track that displays our intentions and reactions. In fact, one of the features that set humans apart from other primates is that we have developed distinct "whites" to our eyes, a characteristic that even our closest relatives, the apes, do not possess. Making the direction of our glance all the more conspicuous, these "whites" have enabled us to develop an entire "glance language," with which we both send and receive messages, some of them amazingly subtle.

What are the rules of gaze behavior in our own culture? One of the most apparent is that while we're speaking, we rarely make eye contact with our listener. Our eyes are the primary receptors of outside stimuli, and while we're trying to form our thoughts, we often find it necessary to block out signals that might distract, confuse, or interrupt us. It's when we *do* look—at the end of a statement or question, at grammatical breaks—that these signals provide periodic feedback on our listener's reactions to what we're saying.

Does he understand—nodding ever so slightly, blinking periodically? Is he bewildered—brows lowered, eyes staring dully or "fogged up"? Does he agree—eyes wide and bright, with an occasional "mm-hmm"? Have we aroused feelings of protest, disgust, or even horror—eyes looking away as he tries to rationalize or modify what we've said? Is he paying careful attention—eyes quickly blinking? Is he bored—eyes roaming distractedly or perhaps even fixed in a zombie-like gaze? If he blinks once involuntarily, he's surprised. And if his gaze keeps darting to some distant object, he's growing anxious or impatient.

While we're collecting this information, we're also transmitting our own eye signals, a whole range of cues that act as "traffic lights" to the flow of conversation.

One example of this "eye punctuation" is the eye-flash, a psychologists' term for a sudden widening of the eyes to emphasize a point. Often accompanying the eye-flash is the eyebrow-flash, an equally quick lifting of the brows that adds even stronger emphasis to the point we're making. This gesture is also a universal sign of greeting and flirtation, as was demonstrated by a German behavioral scientist, Irenäus Eibl-Eibesfeldt, who traveled throughout the world with a camera-and-mirrors device, making candid films of people. He found that even among such diverse peoples as the Balinese, the French, and the Papuans, a common gesture when two people met was a rapid raising and lowering of the eyebrows (about one-sixth of a second—so short a time that the effect is more subliminal than conscious), accompanied by a smile and perhaps a slight nod.

One of the most common conversational signals is the terminal glance, a slightly longer-than-normal meeting of our listener's eyes to signal that we are about to finish our statement or question and are ready to yield the floor. Some eye behaviorists call this signal the "full-stop" glance, since we are in effect placing an ocular "period" at the end of our sentence or thought. With a slight upward note in our voice, a brightening of the eyes, a lifting of one or both brows, the full-stop easily becomes a question mark.

If we have several listeners, we can use this glance to direct a general question or comment to a particular person without actually saying his name, or simply to designate who will speak next. So important is this signal that if we inadvertently omit it, our listener may not realize it's his turn to speak, and an awkward silence may follow. A person who's adept at "eye power" will use this phenomenon to his advantage by avoiding eye contact with members of his audience and gracefully retaining his hold on the spotlight. Watch for these conversation monopolizers, from the popular raconteur at your next party to the attention- and power-grabber at your next business meeting.

Breaking the Rules

These rules are all part of the "normal" pattern. How people break them—and these, like any other rules, are meant to be broken—gives us special insights into their personalities and situations, insights that words alone usually cannot provide. One example is that, while speaking, abstract thinkers look more and sustain more eye contact than the average person because of their greater ability to integrate visual stimuli without risking "information overload" and becoming distracted or confused. Similarly, the more deeply involved two people are in their discussion, the more they are able to look at each other and keep the conversation running smoothly.

The late Ralph Exline, while a psychologist at the University of Delaware, conducted dozens of experiments to determine patterns of gaze behavior. One of his findings was that looking is also directly related to liking; in other words, "the more you like, the more you look." When someone hears something that pleases him, his eyes will probably shift immediately to the speaker. Watch two people who are happily reunited after a long period apart; their long, almost thirsty gazes seem to be trying to make up for the couple's not seeing each other—for "lost looking," as it were—by looking more now.

In his book *The Psychology of Interpersonal Behavior,* British social psychologist Michael Argyle writes that when looking goes over the 60-percent mark, the two people are probably more interested in each other than in their actual conversation. One might say their eyes are having a quiet conversation of their own. When the interest *isn't* equal for both partners, a conflict of signals may occur. A prolonged gaze that might have been considered flattering now becomes soulful "sheep's eyes" or even lecherous leering—annoying or unsettling signals when the feeling isn't mutual.

Gender itself is an important influence on the amount of looking we do. In one of his experiments, Ralph Exline created groups of three women or three men and, in order to get them involved in active conversation, asked each group to discuss possible names for a hypothetical new laundry detergent. The students were unaware that their visual interaction was being observed from behind a one-way mirror.

Women, it was found, make eye contact more than men do, and once they have made this eye contact, they hold it longer. But these results applied only to same-sex gaze interaction. Would they hold true for mixed pairs?

Two years later Exline published the results of an experiment that answered this question. This time male and female students were interviewed individually by either a man or a woman. The interviewer kept his or her eyes fixed on the subject during the entire length of the interview, so that any eye contact the subject made was actual eye contact with the interviewer. The subjects' behavior was observed from behind a one-way mirror.

Once again, the women did more looking than the men—while speaking, while listening, and even during the informal discussion that took place when the interview was supposedly over.

Since this experiment, a number of variations have been conducted, with similar, if more subtle, results. As might be expected, both men and women look more when they're with someone they like, though men do their extra looking while they're listening, and women do theirs while they're speaking. But why, in general, do women look more than men? One explanation relates to the way society trains men and women to behave according to their sexual "roles." Supposedly, men are the more unemotional ones, strong, silent, and rather passive, while women are expected to make the effort to be more affectionate and communicate their warmth. One easy way of doing this is to make more eye contact. Also, a woman may be unconsciously conditioned to seek approval of her behavior from men, and increased looking is one indication that this approval-need is present. This would also explain women's increased looking while speaking; they crave more feedback on what they're saying, especially if men—again, behaving according to *their* sexual "role"—do not fully express their emotions and responses. In another experiment, in which men and women spoke on the telephone, the women spoke less than they had in person—possible further evidence that they are uncomfortable when they cannot get visual feedback. The men, on the other hand, spoke more, perhaps because they felt more comfortable away from the women's searching gazes.

As we mentioned, we look more when we crave approval or liking, or if, as the psychologists put it, we are high in need-affiliation. Often called the "love motive," need-affiliation is the instinctive desire to form warm, intimate relationships, a desire each of us has to some degree. You'll know people who are high in need-affiliation not only by their abnormally long gazes but also by the earnest, searching look in their eyes, a look that seems to say, "Please like me."

Even in formalized situations, the amount of looking is a key to approval and disapproval between people. At the University of California in Riverside, Dr. Stephen S. Fugito conducted an experiment to test the generally accepted rule that when a person expects or desires approval from someone, he increases his eye contact with that person.

Dr. Fugito set up a number of interviews between students and interviewers. The interviewers were of varying status in relation to the students, and were instructed to behave in either an approving or a disapproving manner.

The results showed that when we talk to someone, whatever his relative status, we tend to look at him more, and make eye contact more often, if we crave and expect to receive his approval. If this approval is indeed shown, the amount of looking increases further.

Ironically, looking also increases when our tempers flare and we become defensive, aggressive, or hostile, as if in our heightened assertiveness we are not afraid to let our eyes show emotions we might otherwise hide. And, in the increased rhythm of the argument, we need to look more often into our opponent's eyes to read *his* ever-changing flow of emotions and attitudes.

The Laws of Look-Away

What do we signal by looking *less?* Aside from averting our gaze when we're concentrating, we often turn our eyes away to conceal reactions and feelings from our partners. The old belief that we hide our eyes in guilt, embarrassment, or shame is not far wrong; Darwin even saw it as a subconscious attempt to disappear. Like the proverbial ostrich who thinks that if he doesn't look he won't be seen, we believe that if we can't see the other person—or the truth or accusation in his eyes— he can't hurt us. After Adam and Eve had eaten from the Tree of Knowledge, they hid themselves and would not look upon God, thinking they could thus escape his wrath.

A number of experiments have been performed to see whether eye contact is indeed connected with cheating and lying, or "Machiavellianism"—skepticism about human nature, willingness to use deceit to get one's way, belief in manipulation. In one of the most famous experiments, Ralph Exline told pairs of students that they were to be tested in group decision-making. Each pair was shown a series of playing cards and asked to come to a decision on a guess as to what was on the reverse side of each. The experimenter would record their guesses and pretend to compare them to the correct answers, but in actuality the experiment was intended to test something quite different. For in each pair, one student was actually a confederate of the experimenter.

Halfway through the experiment, the experimenter would be called out of the room. While he was gone, his confederate would involve the other student in cheating by reading the experimenter's answer sheet. Some of the students participated willingly; others refused to be more than innocent bystanders.

When the experimenter returned and resumed showing the cards, he expressed increasing skepticism about the pair's high percentage of correct answers, until he finally accused them outright of cheating. The hapless students had earlier filled out a questionnaire on their Machiavellian tendencies, and their eye behavior now showed that the low Machiavellians looked away while trying to protect their cheating partners. The high Machiavellians intentionally made even more eye contact with the experimenter to conceal their deceit, and this eye contact increased even further as the interrogation proceeded.

But, according to a popular song, "You can't hide your lying eyes," a statement that has been confirmed by a number of psychologists. One is Paul Ekman, who in 1953 began experiments to investigate the meanings of patients' nonverbal behavior during group therapy. In his headquarters at San Francisco's Langley Porter Neuropsychiatric Institute, Ekman performed one of his best-known experiments, testing the ability of a person to lie not only with words but also with the body.

First he showed a group of student nurses a rather bland piece of film, asked them to describe it honestly, and videotaped their descriptions. Then he showed them a film of someone who had been badly burned. At the end of this disturbing film, subtitles appeared on the screen instructing the nurses to describe it dishonestly—as if it had been about flowers or children playing (or, in other words, as bland as the first film)—to another person, who had not seen the film or the nurses' faces as they watched it. These descriptions were also videotaped, and then compared to the descriptions of the first film.

In almost all cases, Ekman's team of trained face-readers were able to tell when the nurses were lying by a number of subtle nonverbal clues, one of which was their eye language. Though they might smile and try to make more eye contact to disguise their lies, their eyes still darted away a greater number of times, and they often gave themselves away by gazing for unnaturally long periods.

Under normal circumstances, however, we avoid making eye contact while we're speaking. Some people find it difficult to make any eye contact at all. An acutely shy person, for instance, cannot bear to communicate on the eyes' intimate level. The penetrating honesty in other people's eyes delves painfully deep into his basic insecurity; he cannot risk revealing what he believes is a low self-worth by letting people read it in his eyes.

In his book *Shyness,* Philip Zimbardo observes that in addition to their reluctance to speak, many shy people reveal their phobia of contact with people through their frequent inability to look someone in the eye. "For some," he writes, "making eye contact with a stranger is a formidable barrier. They feel uncomfortable when the contact is more intense or prolonged than 'is called for.'" Many psychologists recommend that parents of shy children get down to their child's level or pick him up to theirs in order to make better eye contact and help the child become accustomed to this interaction early in life.

The absence of this eye contact between parent and child may, in fact, be responsible not only for shyness but for other childhood and adult maladjustments as well. (Michael Argyle even suggests that schizophrenia and autism may result partly from a lack of this bonding in infancy.) One of the main reasons primates use gaze as an affiliation signal is that primate infants and mothers are able to look at each other during breast-feeding; in fact, primates are the only mammals in which nursing fosters this eye contact. Human babies, for example, can focus at a distance of 8 to 12 inches, approximately the distance of the mother's face when she holds the infant to nurse. By the third week of life babies smile at a nodding head; by the fifth week they can exchange mutual glances. They also show a pleasurable response (smiles and pupil dilation) to eyes and eye patterns. By the fifth or sixth month, the child identifies its mother's smiling face as belonging to one particular person; it is at this time that a close bond develops and begins to strengthen as the child grows. All during the first year, the child and the parent typically play many mutual-gaze games, such as peekaboo, that are among the child's first experiences in social communication. This close bonding will continue through the growing-up years, when the mother's face will be the first place the child turns when he's in trouble.

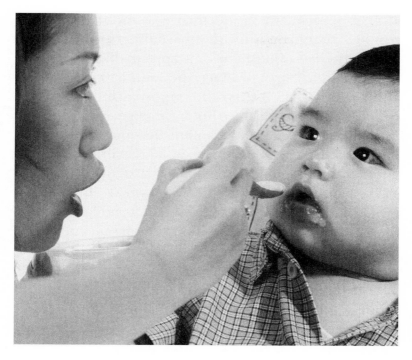

Ocular bonding between mother and child is one of the first and most crucial ways in which eye language establishes our psychological identity as adults.

In experiments performed with monkeys, infants reared without contact with their mothers showed little interest in the opposite sex; it appears likely that this lack of contact may produce the same effect on some humans. To demonstrate the importance of this early visual bonding, psychologists have experimented with "imprinting," in which an infant becomes attached to the dominant moving object in its environment and does its best to follow that object around. Dogs and ducks have thus been bonded to humans, human babies to wolves; there is evidence that a similar imprinting takes place between human infants and their mothers. Babies smile when they see their mother's face or her smile, or when they make eye contact with her; the baby's eyes follow the mother around the room. All through our lives the face of our mother (or whomever we are bonded to) acts as a stimulus by arousing certain sentiments within us. For many people these sentiments are refuge, warmth, understanding, rescue, relief. Could we be recalling one of our earliest associations, that of the soothing nourishment of our mother's milk, with the image of her face as we nursed? And are bottle-fed babies, who do not necessarily experience that frequent 8-to-12-inch eye contact, deprived of this sort of psychological mother-bonding?

In our own culture, where so much emphasis is placed on gaze behavior—looking someone in the eye—along with the inability to make eye contact comes a whole set of related problems in such areas as communication, assertiveness, sexual intimacy, and self-esteem. In other cultures this may not be the case. In

Japan, for instance, the accepted gaze behavior is for a speaker to focus on his listener's neck. Little use is made of the facial-visual channel to either send or receive information, and much of the communication is through nuances of spoken language and body position. (A good explanation for the Japanese paying little attention to eyes is that Japanese mothers carry their infants on their backs much of the time, and have little visual contact with the child's face; in effect, the gaze-bonding is never really formed.) Thus, for the Japanese, the absence of eye contact is virtually not a problem at all.

Other Games, Other Rules

Within our culture there are people who follow their own, and often quite extreme, rules of gaze behavior. Whether they are constantly staring or avoid eye contact altogether, they are probably suffering serious psychological problems.

For example, depressives and neurotics tend to avert their gaze when interviewed about their problems, as do schizophrenics. Psychoanalyst Alexander Lowen, in his book *The Language of the Body,* observes: "It is in his eyes that the schizophrenic shows most clearly his illness. One can make the diagnosis, at times, from the eyes alone." They are "off," "blank," "vacant," "out of touch." Wilhelm Reich said they have a "typical faraway look of remoteness. . . . It seems as if the psychotic looks right through you with an absentminded but deep look into far distances." One of the goals of therapists helping these patients to readjust is to teach them to look at other people without making them feel threatened or uncomfortable with a long stare. By making a conscious effort, the patient learns to obtain necessary visual information without excessive staring.

On the other hand, autistic children—those seemingly absorbed in their private fantasies—do the least gazing. They are, in fact, so afraid of making eye contact that gaze aversion is one important criterion of diagnosis. These children peek at others in quick, darting glances, often through their fingers, or they will avoid looking altogether by turning their backs or pulling hats over their heads. Oddly, it is not social contact they avoid, but simply eyes and faces; they will sit happily on an adult's lap but avert his or her gaze.

One explanation for this gaze aversion is that, possibly due to a genetic defect, autistic children are abnormally susceptible to arousal of the cerebral cortex—the outer layer of the brain's cerebrum, where conscious mental processes take place. Since mutual gaze is arousing, they avoid eye contact to eliminate this sensory stimulation and thus keep their levels of arousal low enough not to disturb their inner world.

Even "normal" rules of gaze behavior can create problems when a person from one culture visits or moves to another in which the rules are different. While in our own culture a direct meeting of someone's eyes is a sign of honesty or assertiveness, in Latin America children are trained to lower their eyes to show respect for their superiors. Thus, in an American school, a Puerto Rican child's averted gaze intended to signal obedience to a teacher may be misinterpreted as a gesture of defiance, slyness, or guilt. There is even the case of the boy who, when his teacher tried to establish a rapport by forcing the boy to look him in the face, fled from the school in panic.

Similar rules of nonlooking take the form of taboos in various parts of the world. Navaho children are taught not to look directly at another person during conversation, and among the Bororo and Wituto Indians of South America both speaker and listener keep their eyes fixed on irrelevant objects. Even more extreme is the storyteller who turns away from his audience to face the back of the hut.

A Luo man of Kenya must not look at his mother-in-law. In Sierra Leone, the Mende people believe that the dead reappear in human guise and can be recognized by their inability to look a live person in the face. Naturally the Mende are suspicious of gaze-averters. And in many parts of the Far East, eye contact during conversation is a serious breach of etiquette.

On the other hand, in some cultures the eyes are vital channels of communication, since the rest of the body is covered with cloths and veils. One example is the nomadic Tuaregs of North Africa, who stare steadily at each other during conversation in order to exchange as much information as possible.

An extensive study of culture variations in gaze patterns was conducted by O. Michael Watson at the University of Colorado. Pairs of male foreign students were asked to converse on any subject in their native language while researchers observed from behind one-way mirrors. The subject's "visual style" was scored on a scale of 1 (focusing sharply on the other person's eyes) to 4 (no eye contact at all; looking down or gazing into space). Watson found that regardless of how much time the students had spent in the United States, the cultural gaze patterns they learned in childhood still held fast. Men from "contact cultures," where people typically stand close together and frequently touch each other (Arab countries, Latin America, Southern Europe) had an average score of 2.41; "noncontact cultures" (Asia, India-Pakistan, Northern Europe), an average of 3.45. Looking, then, might be considered another form of touching, of getting closer to someone.

Breaking the Gaze Barrier

If gaze is so important a part of social exchange, what happens when we can't see each other while speaking? Without the additional—and often more accurate— communication of the eyes, are our messages unclear or incomplete? Is verbal communication enough?

Many experimenters have compared people's responses to face-to-face encounters, communication by videophone, and communication by telephone. They have found that although people miss visual signals and prefer to see each other's faces while speaking, the absence of gaze is not as serious an inhibitor as one might imagine. The reason is that over several generations of telephone-talking we have replaced eye-punctuation with a system of audible signals—feedback sounds we make while the other person is talking—that express agreement ("mm-hmm" or "uh-huh"), disagreement ("unh-unh"), doubt ("hmmm . . ."), or simply that we are still listening ("mmm").

Sometimes the absence of visual signals is an advantage. Studies have shown that it is easier to change someone's opinion over the telephone than in a face-to-face encounter—especially when the opinion being argued is not personal but based on official (such as corporate) policy or data. Without the extraneous distraction of gaze signals, negotiators are able to concentrate more completely on the hard facts of their argument and present a stronger case.

In most social situations, however, in-person encounters are far more effective, and two people meeting for the first time will probably like each other more if they introduce themselves with the benefit of the eyes' character- and warmth-conveying signals than if they first speak over the telephone. When the video-phone comes into common use in our homes, we can look forward to more enjoyable and satisfying encounters (though we may feel less need to meet our friends in person). In our workplaces this invention has increased the amount of personal fulfillment we get from business transactions but decreased our effectiveness, for as we've seen, we're swayed more easily when we can read our partner's eye signals. Business communications are becoming more personal, more prolonged, and, inevitably, less businesslike.

An eye-language barrier far simpler than the telephone is dark sunglasses, which make it impossible to read the subtler messages and conversation signals in our partner's eyes. The stereotypical Hollywood celebrities famous for wearing them know that most unwanted conversations with strangers begin with simple eye contact. By hiding their eyes behind these one-way windows, they avoid making this contact, without the risk of offending fans (who would otherwise see them look quickly away) or hurting their own reputations. People often wear sunglasses when they want to depart from the accepted rules of eye contact. They can stare, look away, or meet others' glances without detection or obligation, passing among us in virtual anonymity. The irony, though, is that most of us get the uncomfortable feeling that eyes behind dark glasses turned in our general direction are staring at us relentlessly, and we look away accordingly.

Most of us dislike talking to someone who's wearing sunglasses. When we can't read the other person's reactions and directional signals, conversation becomes awkward. Especially disturbing are mirrored sunglasses, which present not an impersonal dark surface but a reflection of our *own* eyes. These mirrors upset the entire exchange, and we get the confusing impression that we are both speaker and listener.

Even very strong eyeglasses can interfere with the smooth sending and receiving of the eyes' conversational messages, since they distort the appearance of the eyes. Some people solve this problem by replacing their "Coke bottle" glasses with contact lenses, which correct vision without creating any barriers to the other person's reading of the eyes. This "cosmetic" reason— letting the eyes speak their language more clearly and dramatically—is in fact the most common one for switching from glasses to contacts.

How do we react when the barrier is not hidden eyes but too many of them? If we are giving a lecture or speaking to a large audience, we look down from the lectern into a sea of staring eyes, feel threatened or self-conscious, and instinctively look at none of them; we stare too long at our notes, gaze out across space at the rear wall of the auditorium. Experienced speakers know they can make their addresses more effective by simulating one-to-one gaze behavior as closely as possible. From time to time they force themselves to look directly at individuals in the audience—a technique that allows each listener to believe subconsciously that he is the only one. Without this simulated one-to-one eye contact, listeners feel ignored, as if their presence made no difference. Accordingly, they may consciously resist the speaker, grow bored, or simply not listen at all.

On the other hand, what if the "audience" is not a sea of eyes but one glaring one—a television camera? Television newscasters read their copy from a device over the camera called an Autocue, on which the words roll slowly past. It would of course be easiest for the newscaster to gaze continuously at the camera, reading his lines. But his steady stare, he knows, is disturbing to viewers, who soon become more occupied by the stare than by the news itself. Therefore the newscaster gives himself an excuse to look away as he would in a one-to-one conversation: a sheaf of papers to which he can conveniently "refer." Watch for the inexperienced newscasters who stare too often or too long at the camera, as if they were able to retain huge chunks of copy without looking back at their papers. Their delivery is unnatural and less effective because they are not yet adept at simulating everyday conversational gaze behavior as closely as they should. The veteran newscasters, and any others who must appear to address a television audience in an impromptu manner, treat the camera as if it were another person, and their words have as much impact on us as if this were actually the case.

We've now seen barriers to reading eye signals and other barriers to sending them. The ultimate barrier combines them both: blindness. A blind person must conduct all of his encounters without reading the signals in his partner's eyes. He must extract as much meaning as possible from what he hears, and he may shift his head in order to let this especially well-developed sense tune in to subtleties of word choice, intonation, and inflection. These are, in effect, the same qualities we rely on to understand a speaker fully on the telephone.

In face-to-face encounters, however, the blind person is at an additional disadvantage. The late Erving Goffman, in his book *Stigma,* writes: ". . . the blind person's failure to direct his face to the eyes of his co-participant is an event that repeatedly violates communication etiquette and repeatedly disrupts the feedback mechanics of spoken interaction." Aware that his eyes may be sending misleading or disturbing signals, the blind person may take to wearing dark glasses, feeling it is better that his unseeing eyes not be seen.

Eye Tests

To learn more about the eyes' power to send messages simply by their pattern of looking and not looking, perform some experiments of your own, preferably on friends with whom your eye exchanges are generally normal. Try keeping your eyes lowered throughout an entire conversation, making fleeting contact only rarely. Chances are your friend will ask what's bothering you, what you're keeping from him. For variation, look away repeatedly while you're talking; your friend will probably ask you what's the matter, what's on your mind, or if you're in a hurry.

Try some ocular flattery: While your friend is talking, keep your eyes fixed avidly on his face, blink rapidly, and smile when appropriate. You'll be surprised at his increased enthusiasm as he responds to your "all eyes" look.

Finally, set up some gaze-barriers. The simplest is to place your hands over your eyes, as if you're rubbing or resting them. It's likely that after a while your friend will show signs of discomfort at being deprived of the "visual track," and he may even ask you to take your hands away from your eyes, just as we might ask someone to take his fingers out of his mouth so that we can hear him clearly.

Try wearing sunglasses during a conversation. Indoors especially, where these glasses are an obvious eye-shield, people feel at a disadvantage and will usually avoid looking at the glasses, assuming but never *really* knowing that the hidden eyes are fixed unwaveringly on them. Here, too, your friend is likely to ask you to remove the barrier—to take the glasses off.

In this chapter we've concerned ourselves primarily with the rather basic messages we send and receive by either looking or not looking at various times during a conversation. But just as important as *where* our eyes look is *how* they look. Studies have shown that the first feature we look at in a stranger is his eyes, and the ways in which the shape, size, and color of those eyes (not to mention brows, lashes, and lines) influence our perception of that person's character have fascinated experts and laymen for hundreds of years. As we'll see in the following chapter, from this fascination has developed an amazingly accurate set of findings about the connection between personality and the *physical* eye.

2

THE PHYSICAL EYE

A Guide to Physiognomy

*Thine eyes are like the deep, blue boundless heaven
Contracted to two circles underneath
Their long, fine lashes; dark, far, measureless,
Orb within orb, and line through line inwoven.*

—Percy Bysshe Shelley, *Prometheus Unbound*

It is only shallow people who do not judge by appearances.

—Oscar Wilde, *The Picture of Dorian Gray*

Judging by Appearances

There is much more to eye language than how we look and do not look during a conversation. Even before the looking, before the countless types of gazes and glances we send each other, there are the eyes themselves—the size of the pupils, the color of the iris, the whiteness of the "whites," the size and slant of the eyes, the lashes, the brows, and the lines, moles, and other markings around the eyes.

When two pairs of eyes meet, it is the physical appearance of those eyes that registers first. In surveys in which people have been asked what they look at first in a stranger, the answer given most often was "the eyes." Prove it to yourself; pick up any newspaper or magazine and glance at the pictures of people's faces. If you're like most people, you look first at the eyes, and though they're not moving, they're giving you a whole personality profile of the person they belong to.

There are warm eyes and cold eyes, wise eyes, strong eyes, and eyes full of mystery. The eyes of Anne Frank gaze beseechingly out at us, wide and glistening and full of young wonder at the beauty of the world. Joseph Goebbels glares out at us from deep, dark sockets, eyes that look as if they never smiled. In Albert Einstein's eyes we see the depth of his understanding of the world; in the lines around them, the light-years his experience seems to have encompassed. Churchill's eyes seem to defy the world. Mona Lisa has eyes so hauntingly enticing they follow us around the room. And all this from a photograph, a painting. Needless to say, we take similar eye-readings of the people we encounter every day—a whole world of signals before our glances even meet, if they meet at all.

Physiognomy: A Brief History

As you might suspect, eye-reading is nothing new. It's as old, in fact, as mankind itself.

The practice of reading character from the features of the face—the science of physiognomy—has long been a part of our quest to understand ourselves, beginning with the early humans, who began to link smiles, frowns, and grimaces with certain personality traits. This is a natural association, when we consider that it is our facial expressions that register our strongest emotions, and that facial formations affect these expressions. According to the *Funk & Wagnalls New Standard Encyclopedia,* "The art is founded upon the belief, which has long and generally prevailed, that there is an intimate connection between the features and expression of the face and the qualities and habits of the mind."

Around 340 B.C., Aristotle continued the work of Hippocrates by writing *Physiognomonica,* believed to be the oldest treatise on physiognomy as well as a forerunner of modern medicine. In this work he wrote:

> When men have large foreheads, they are slow to move; when they have broad ones, they are apt to be distraught. Men with small foreheads are fickle, whereas if they are rounded or bulging out the owners are quick-tempered. Straight eyebrows indicate softness of disposition; brows curving toward the nose are a sign of harshness; brows drawn together mean jealousy; those that curve out toward the temples, humor and dissimulation. The staring eye indicates impudence, the winking indecision. Large and outstanding ears indicate a tendency to irrelevant talk or chattering.

Note the emphasis Aristotle placed on the appearance of the eyes and brows.

A story in the Talmud tells of a king who sent his court painter to capture the likeness of Moses so that his wise men could analyze this famous face and explain what made Moses so great. Though there's no record of whether the king's plan was successful, we do know that similar analyses were attempted on Socrates, Alexander, and a number of other ancient greats.

In the fifth century B.C., the Chinese of Confucius' time were reading faces as indicators of their owners' personalities. Later, two centuries before the birth of Christ, physiognomists of the Chin and Han dynasties put into clever verse the Points on the Map of the Face (each of one hundred locations represented a year in the subject's life) and would recite the appropriate rhymes as they read the faces of their clients. The emperor, the general, the villager—all subscribed to this science that centuries of practice had proven sound.

The chieftains of ancient Africa and the monarchs of medieval Europe recognized the body's ability to reveal character, and dressed to cover every inch of themselves so as not to reveal weaknesses to potential rivals or adversaries.

The true founder of physiognomy is considered to be Johann Kaspar Lavater (1741–1801), a Swiss poet, mystic, and writer on philosophy and theology. With his keen powers of observation, a scientifically inquiring mind, and a poet's imagination, Lavater became convinced that even the subtlest of human traits could be determined from the features of individual faces. He believed that the features were shaped not only by air, environment, diet, and occupation but also by particular habits of thinking and psychological qualities. In his pioneer work, *Essays in Physiognomy,* published in 1789 and including contributions by Goethe and Herder, Lavater used an impressive array of depictions of the human face to explain how to discern temperament from appearance. "He who has a daring eye tells downright truths and downright lies," he wrote, and gave instructions for reading character traits from the eyes in relation to the profile, eye color, the shape and openness of the eyes and the distance between them, and even the heaviness, shape, and closeness of the eyebrows. The British essayist John Saunders also believed that the eyes were the nucleus of this study, and wrote in his essay "Physiognomy":

> Whatever of goodness emanates from the soul gathers its soft halo in the eyes: and if the heart be the lurking-place of crime, the eyes are sure to betray the secret. A beautiful eye makes silence eloquent, a kind eye makes contradiction assent, an enraged eye makes beauty a deformity.

The 1800s saw the zenith of both physiognomy and the allied science of phrenology, the reading of character from the "bumps" of the head. Many popular guides appeared, and the reading of both facial features and head shapes became a craze throughout Europe.

It was not until the 1930s that physiognomy again became the subject of serious research. Dr. Werner Wolff began this work in Berlin and Spain, and American psychologists first learned of it through Dr.

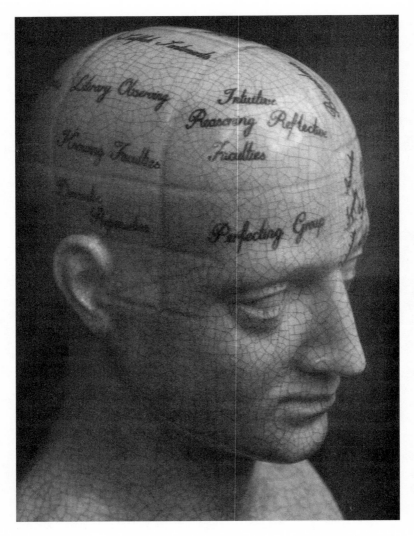

In the nineteenth century, eye-reading was an aspect of phrenology, a branch of physiognomy in which character was read from the bumps of the head and face. This model shows the locations of the mental functions.

Gordon W. Allport of Harvard, and P. E. Vernon. Eventually Wolff came to teach at Bard College and Columbia University, and carried his research into the 1940s. By this time his book *Physiognomy,* a study of emotional, temperamental, and characterological makeup that had received considerable financial backing by Germany's researchers in *Gestalten* (configurations, including those of facial expressions), had sparked the interest of other psychologists in America. Unfortunately, by 1940 psychologists and psychiatrists had all but lost interest in physiognomy, for newer disciplines such as behaviorism, psychoanalysis, and Rorschach were just coming to the fore.

State of the Art

But despite the decline of formalized feature-reading, one need only think a moment to realize that we have never stopped making at least a subconscious connection between appearance and character. As children we knew that witches had long, pointed noses and warts; angels had serene faces and shimmering golden hair. As grown-ups we recognize a variety of "types," from the person with patrician or aristocratic features to the "Neanderthal."

Pick up any classic work of fiction and note the influence of physiognomy on the way writers described their characters. Chaucer, Balzac, the Brontës, Dickens, Conan Doyle—all made their characters "look like" their personalities, so that appearance was usually a clue to true motivations.

In our day-to-day lives we look at strangers and draw certain conclusions about their personalities even before they move or speak. "She has a weak chin (and a weak personality?)." "He has an artist's hands (and an artist's talent?)." "Her eyes are too close together; I don't trust her." "With feet that big, he must be clumsy." "Her hawk nose says she's greedy."

The producers of films and plays are acutely aware of the often unconscious connections we make between appearance and character, and the casting of actors is often largely dependent on their "looking" the part.

So aware are we of the personality statements our appearances make that we invest in "remedies" for presumed defects, from lipstick to contact lenses to plastic surgery. We may further change ourselves to suit the personality we think we have, wish we had, or want others to think we have: hair is transplanted, curled, straightened or dyed; eyebrows are darkened, thinned, or reshaped; eyelashes are thickened or applied; skin is powdered, tanned, or bleached; teeth are capped or replaced; weight is lost and gained. And we may conceal features that we feel make false statements about our personalities: scarves or high-necked dresses to hide neck wrinkles, hats or toupees over balding pates, dark glasses to mask bags under the eyes.

In New York City, which once boasted a society of practicing physiognomists, the personnel departments of some of the world's largest and most sophisticated companies are hiring face-readers to teach their recruiters to read potential employees' features during interviews. With their time at a premium, recruiters need to learn as much about applicants as they can in the shortest possible time. Face-reading is the answer.

Doctors have even conducted experiments to confirm that eye color is firmly linked to behavior and personality. Someday, they claim, people in jobs requiring certain specialized qualities may be selected after their eye coloring has been taken into consideration.

A number of experts have studied feature-reading, from W. H. Sheldon, who during World War II defined three basic body types and the temperaments that go with them, to a California lawyer who revived the predictive aspects of physiognomy in a system called "personology." From years of watching people in the courtroom, the attorney claimed that he could make accurate predictions about an individual's behavior from physiognomic clues alone.

Consciously or unconsciously, we are all feature-readers. Aside from the people we encounter from day to day, with the flourishing of the visual media—from newspapers, books, and magazines to film, television, video, and the Internet—we are provided with an endless variety of facial types to study, compare, and learn from. And always the focal point of our observations is the eyes and the area around them.

To help you apply the secrets of physiognomists past and present, here is a guide to the interpretation of the strictly physical eye, beginning with the irises and moving outward.

An Eye-Reading Manual

The Irises

The first factor to study is the size of the iris in proportion to the "whites" on either side, below, and sometimes, above. Physiognomists have found that persons with small irises ("beady eyes") tend to hide their emotions and be perpetually unhappy with the state of their lives. They are often complainers or rebels, or their bitterness toward the Establishment (which keeps them from realizing their goals) may cause them to drop out of society altogether, outcasts, loners, or even criminals. If, on the other hand, they are more determined to reach their goals, they are not above using force or cruelty to do so, especially if they have "three-white-sided" eyes (see "The Whites," below).

People with large irises, on the other hand, are more adaptable to their life stations and surroundings. They are also, however, averse to change, which makes them unreliable in emergencies; they tend to make unwise decisions. Generally, the large-irised individual is affectionate and family-oriented, thinking with the heart rather than the head. He is gentle, calm, sympathetic, and of a conservative nature, often an oversensitive person who tends to take too many things personally.

Now make note of the color of the irises. This factor is, of course, determined hereditarily; however, physiognomists believe not only that our characteristics affect our appearance, but also that our appearance can affect our characteristics. Some scientists have seconded this belief by forwarding the theory that the color of the pigment in the eye may even affect different areas of the brain (the eye is, in fact, virtually an exposed extension of this organ) and so *influence* behavior and personality!

In the December 1978 issue of *Science Digest,* Michael Phillips reported on an unusual experiment in his article "Eye Color: A Personality Guide." Two specialists in human behavior, Dr. John Glover and Dr. A. L. Gary, had given a series of psychological tests to groups of light-eyed and dark-eyed children at the Chattanooga Institute of Human Studies, and found that, in general, the darker the irises, the tougher the personality and yet the more extreme the reactions to danger or a crisis. People with dark irises hold up better under pressure and utilize more energy and inventiveness in solving a problem, yet if a project becomes tedious they are more likely than people with light irises to drop it. Light irises indicate staying power, the ability to apply oneself and consider a problem carefully. Among the children tested by Drs. Glover and Gary, those with light irises were also more widely read and could retain information from books and other sources more effectively.

On a more specific level, the actual color of the iris indicates additional traits. Here are some capsule characterizations, drawn not only from the findings of Drs. Glover and Gary but also from the writings of ancient physiognomists in both Europe and the Orient. Interestingly, they all pretty much agree.

Brown

Maiden! with the meek brown eyes.

—Henry Wadsworth Longfellow, *Maidenhood*

If your irises are brown, yours is a two-sided personality: on one side, steadfastness, practicality, and a strong sense of commitment; on the other, vivacity and a rare affability that may make you seem rather freewheeling. When the brown is especially dark, the vital, outgoing side predominates; light brown tilts the scales toward a more serious, self-sufficient person, an individualist with a retiring nature.

Hazel

Thou wilt quarrel with a man for cracking nuts, having no other reason but because thou hast hazel eyes: what eye but such an eye would spy out such a quarrel?

—William Shakespeare, *Romeo and Juliet*

Irises that hover almost exactly between brown and green (the color commonly called "hazel") indicate that you possess a virtually boundless inner vitality. Yours is a determined, vigorous personality—imaginative, always ready for an adventure, and courageous when trouble looms ahead; look out, however, for a decidedly selfish streak. Balancing these qualities are your sense of responsibility and awareness of your limitations. You are a profound thinker with an uncommon sensitivity to outside stimuli, especially colors.

Green

Her eyes were as green as leeks.

—William Shakespeare, *A Midsummer-Night's Dream*

If you look upon the world through irises of green, you are a highly unpredictable person with a quiet self-sufficiency that gives you an air of mystery. Gifted with seemingly limitless patience, you are able to exercise restraint of action when necessary or advantageous, and are slow to anger. An intellectual nature combined with exceptional powers of creativity and originality make you especially well suited to the communication fields—especially those with a faster pace, such as television, magazines, and the Internet, since you are able to concentrate even in the most distracting of environments, and perform best under pressure. Physiognomists believe that, in general, green-eyed people are the happiest of the color-groups.

Sea-Green or Emerald

The sea-green mirrors of your eyes . . .
Eyes colored like a water-flower,
And deeper than the green seas' glass.

—Algernon Charles Swinburne, *Félise*

Irises of the deepest green—the green of emeralds or the blue-green of the sea—indicate that you possess all the creative powers of the green-eyed person (see above), but little of the patience. The key word here is unpredictability—yours is a highly impetuous, volatile personality, with a wild temper. Not surprisingly, deep-green irises suggest a sharp edge of nagging envy in your nature, and you are not above using your considerable powers of cunning to get what you want.

Blue

Such a blue inner light from her eyelids outbroke,
You looked at her silence and fancied she spoke.

—Elizabeth Barrett Browning, *My Kate*

There are, of course, various shades of blue, but in general blue irises denote that you possess a high intellect and intelligence. Symbolic of the quest for deeper, higher things, blue combines fervor with sensitivity, which translates into devotion to noble or worthy causes, and a deep sincerity that helps you make friends easily. A cold color, blue also indicates self-sufficiency, though you still recognize the value of cooperative effort. You possess extraordinary stamina but tend to be sentimental and bogged down by routine. Though yours is basically a bright and happy nature, you are often moody and given to bearing grudges.

Dark Blue

How blue were Ariadne's eyes
When, from the sea's horizon line,
At eve, she raised them to the skies!
My Psyche, bluer far than thine.

—Aubrey Thomas de Verre, *Psyche*

Irises of dark blue such as indigo, ultramarine, and cornflower indicate blue's general traits (see above) but replace noble devotion with a more down-to-earth affection. This manifests itself in the helping of others, and in a generally warmer and more approachable personality. Again, watch out for the moodiness—even darker here—that can cloud your true intentions.

Sky Blue

Where did you get your eyes so blue?
Out of the sky as I came through.

—George Macdonald, *At the Back of the North Wind*

Sky blue, the color most frequently associated with the heavens, heightens blue's dedication to noble, lofty causes. You are an unselfish person with a devotion to spiritual attainment while forsaking the material and the worldly.

Light Blue

O lovely eyes of azure,
Clear as the waters of a brook that run
Limpid and laughing in the summer sun.

—Henry Wadsworth Longfellow, *The Masque of Pandora*

Blue irises that are very pale or tinged with gray indicate the same warm and down-to-earth qualities as dark blue, as well as a hardy, active disposition. Also present here, however, is the influence of uncertainty, which may manifest itself in a lack of self-confidence or in un-reasonable fears and phobias.

Violet

And violets, transform'd to eyes,
Inshrined a soul within their blue.

—Thomas Moore, *Evening in Greece*

Rare as an iris color, violet carries an equally rare set of personality traits. As a color of grandeur and impor-tance, it indicates that you are a person with high ideals and an uncompromising perfectionism. You avoid criti-cism and possess great self-esteem, which manifests it-self most often in a sometimes unattractive vanity. There is nothing "shrinking" about your personality.

Yet yours is not an empty vanity. Highly imagina-tive and creative, you possess strong literary, artistic, or dramatic ability; however, once you are aware of your particular genius, you tend to flaunt it, making your vanity all the more irritating.

The key word in describing the violet-eyed person is illusion. Partly as a result of your almost fanatical per-fectionism, you find it necessary to live in a world of your own, preferring to believe that what you do not like simply does not exist.

Violet, color of twilight, of the transition from day to darkness, causes you to yearn for the mystical, to love deeply elaborate ritual.

Perhaps the most important of all the violet-iris traits is charisma. You possess more of it than any other eye-color group, and it allows you to glide happily through life, charming everyone while getting exactly what you want.

Gray

Mine eyes are gray and bright and quick in turning.

—William Shakespeare, *Venus and Adonis*

Generally, gray irises denote obstinacy and courage, but also uncertainty or fickleness in pursuits and affection. But gray is a deceptive color: Though you may appear to be a quiet conformist, even self-effacing, yours is a calculating nature that allows you to wait patiently for an opportunity to press your own interests, possibly at the expense of companions or coworkers.

More specifically, light-gray irises signify an especially fearful personality; medium-gray, false bravado; dark-gray, selfishness.

Black

And yet the large black eyes, like night,
Have passion and have power;
Within their sleepy depths is light,
For some wild wakening hour.

—Letitia Landon, *The Nizam's Daughter*

Irises of black signify a dynamic character: full of energy and inner vitality, hot-tempered, impulsive, and always ready to face dangerous adventures. Your demeanor is one of dignity, without pretention, and commanding respect.

The Whites

Physiognomists read the whites of the eyes as a gauge of both spiritual and general physical status. A person with white showing above and below the pupil is said to have a wild temper, and may actually become violent when angry. A tinge of blue on the white of the eye is the sign of a mystical nature. Health-wise, redness or yellowishness in the whites of the eyes is considered an indication of deteriorated health: The ideal whites are clear and truly white.

For thousands of years the Japanese have made a study of the whites of the eyes, concentrating on a condition they call *sanpaku,* which translated literally means "three" (*san*) "whites" (*paku*). In this condition, the eye presents three white areas around the iris: to each side, and between the iris and the lower lid. *Sanpaku* is said to indicate a serious imbalance in a person's physical, physiological, and spiritual aspects; a person who is out of touch with himself, his body, and the natural forces of the universe. Traditionally, the *sanpaku* has committed sins against the order of the universe and is therefore ill, melancholy, mentally disturbed, and "accident prone." According to Sakurazawa Nyoiti, author of *You Are All Sanpaku, sanpaku* is most of all "a warning, a sign from nature, that one's life is threatened by an early and tragic end." As evidence he names a number of prominent figures whose careers have been cut short by untimely death: Abraham Lincoln, Adolf Hitler, Ngo Dinh Diem, General Abdul Karim Kassem, Marie Antoinette, Archduke Ferdinand, John F. Kennedy, and Marilyn Monroe. Along with *san-paku* come symptoms such as chronic fatigue, low sexual vitality, poor instinctive reactions, bad humor, inability to sleep soundly, and lack of precision in thought and action. The "three-white-sided" person has a restless nature, quickly growing bored with his circumstances in life and rebelling against them; he is also generous and rather careless in matters of money and relationships. The cure, Nyoiti says, can be found in a Far Eastern philosophy and diet which he calls macrobiotics (the first use of the word), based philosophically on the ancient Oriental concept of Yin-Yang forces in the universe, and biochemically on the relationship between sodium and potassium in the body.

As a person approaches death, his irises rise to disclose white above the lower lids; a dead person's irises turn up into his skull. On the other hand, in a healthy newborn baby the lower edge of the irises extends below the lower eyelid, with white areas only to each side of the iris. This is the sign of health, harmony, and well-being both within and without—the state Nyoiti's macrobiotics is said to restore.

In the early 1960s a New York City psychiatrist named Herbert Spiegel discovered another way in which the whites of the eyes "speak" of their owners' psychological workings—specifically, how susceptible they are to being hypnotized. As a clinical professor at Columbia University's College of Physicians and Surgeons, Spiegel noticed that a woman filmed during a trancelike seizure showed an unusual ability to roll her eyes up and down; on the other hand, an unhypnotizable male patient showed no "eye roll" at all. Since then, Spiegel has proven his eye-roll scale to be "a pivotal clinical sign," 75 percent accurate in predicting hypnotizability, by performing the following experiment on over five thousand adults: holding the head level, the subject rolls his eyes upward as far as possible; then, as the subject slowly lowers his eyelids, the amount of white space showing under the irises is measured. Spiegel has found that the greater the white space, the greater the subject's capacity to be hypnotized—as well as his suggestibility and gullibility.

When asked to explain the correlation, Spiegel said, "Hypnosis is a capacity for attentive, receptive concentration that is inherent in a person. Whatever it is in the brain that governs this capacity governs the degree of eye roll." Low scorers ("zeros" and "ones") are not only unhypnotizable but also of an intellectual rather than an emotional nature; wary, critical people who need to control and manipulate others and implement their own plans. "Fours" and "fives," in addition to being highly hypnotizable, live more by their hearts than by their heads, and are creative but uncritically accepting of ideas, trends, and leaders—in other words, they are remarkably childlike and "wide-eyed."

Try the eye-roll test on your family and friends, and have someone test you. It's a little-known key to an important and basic facet of our personalities.

Glitter

We've all experienced firsthand the magic of bright, sparkling eyes—the "flashing" eyes of a Spanish dancer, or the "glow" in the eyes of a person in love. The brilliance of the eye as a gauge of inner vitality—the light, life, or "glitter" of the eye—has been an important facet of Chinese eye-reading for thousands of years.

Without glitter, eyes are dull, spiritless, often glassy, lacking in that spark of intelligence, enthusiasm, and aliveness that others find so attractive. For the Chinese, however, glitter alone is not a reliable index of a person's vitality and emotional health. Also taken into consideration is a person's ability to *concentrate* his gaze, to fix his eyes' glitter on a person or object. This ability is a key to his "control" and "stability."

For example, eyes with glitter that emit concentrated, penetrating rays indicate a powerful character—stable, trustworthy, loyal, and reliable; an achiever. On the other hand, *un*controlled glitter, lacking concentrated power, usually furtive or scattered, denotes a highly changeable personality—unstable, erratic, and emotional. This person may act in a foolhardy or fanatical manner, and his misadventures are likely to prove detrimental to his own career and home life as well as to those around him.

The Eyelids and Lashes

People have always instinctively responded to sleepy, heavy-lidded eyes as sexy—in fact, they're often called "bedroom eyes." Likewise, physiognomists read the eyelids primarily as a gauge of a person's sexuality.

Most apparent is whether the eyelids are plainly visible. If they are, with a fair amount of skin showing over the eye itself, they signify a person who is direct in sexual matters, who states plainly what he wants (or doesn't want) and dislikes wasting time on preliminaries and amenities. Conversely, the person whose eyelids are hidden beneath the bone of the brow is of an analytical approach, constantly weighing and assessing a situation and proceeding slowly toward his goals. Time is no object for this person, though his desires are just as strong as the exposed-eyelid person.

How thick does the upper eyelid appear to be? Thick or heavy lids (not to be confused with swollen) tell of a secret sensuality, a "tiger" in bed. Swollen lids, however, indicate just the opposite: a person who is weary of his present life, low on drive and ambition, without a real purpose, and with minimal interest in affairs of the heart.

Does the upper eyelid droop? In general, this signifies a person with sex appeal, preoccupied with "the chase," but who is apt to be rather cold-hearted—a calculating person whose attempts at feigning warmth or affection give him an air of artificiality.

If the upper eyelid droops only in the middle, it's a sign of maturity and quickness of mind. This person is crafty and often callous, stopping at nothing to achieve his goals.

An upper eyelid drooping from the middle to either the inner or outer corner suggests a person of a pessimistic nature who sometimes lacks initiative and allows himself to be influenced by others.

A drooping lower eyelid is a sign of warmth and sensitivity, of great prowess as a lover; if the drooping is to the right or left the sex drive is especially strong.

If the lower eyelid appears more swollen than drooping, or if there are pronounced eye pouches or "bags" beneath the eyes, the subject may be suffering the physical and psychological effects of an excessive or uncontrolled sex life. This person possesses a pleasant disposition, if perhaps too egocentric; ironically, in nearly all areas besides sex he is seriously lacking in drive.

An incidental but telling factor is the length and thickness of the lashes. Long, full, or curling lashes are the sign of a sensitive, soft-natured person with a love of the spiritual. On the other hand, short, stubby eyelashes belong to practical doers, strongly independent people who are as aggressive as long-lashed people are gentle.

What's Your Eye Type?

Before considering a person's eye type, regard his eyes in terms of their size in relation to his face as a whole, and their position or "slant."

Large eyes are the sign of a sensitive person with a strong sense of the dramatic and a good sense of what's aesthetically pleasing. Strong leadership potential and an attractive personality make the large-eyed person a natural candidate for high corporate positions.

Small eyes signify a shy, introspective nature, a complacent person who finds it difficult to adapt to new people, places, or situations. Though not overly articulate, small-eyed people are apt to be of an intellectual bent, becoming artists or academics. On the romantic side, they are eternally loyal and, when provoked, obsessively jealous.

Are the eyes on a straight line, slanting neither upward nor downward? If so, they are most likely the eyes of a successful person who is in harmony with society—someone who is good-natured, honest, and conscientious.

Upward-slanting eyes belong to a sensitive and intuitive person who knows when to take risks for large returns. Decisions come easily, and danger is rarely seen as an obstacle when following them through.

Downward-slanting eyes, on the other hand, indicate a person who prefers to ingratiate himself to and depend on others rather than plan his own course of action. Optimistic and good-natured, he is easily victimized, especially by members of the opposite sex.

Now take note of the eyes' overall shape. Both the ancient Chinese and the ancient Greeks devised a system of likening people's eyes to the eyes of various animals; oddly enough, the animals' basic "personality" traits were usually apparent in their human eye counterparts. The following is a list of the ten most common eye-shape types, taken from the ancient Chinese physiognomists' list of no less than thirty-nine.

1. Lion eyes are large and strong-looking, almond-shaped, with multiple eyelids both above and below.

Downward-slanting eyes are the sign of a person content to ingratiate himself to others and rely on them to get things done. Optimistic and good-natured, this person is easily victimized, especially by members of the opposite sex.

They denote the lion's reputed sense of fairness and justice, as well as the exceptional leadership skills of a high military, government, or corporate authority.

2. Sheep eyes are extremely long and narrow, with three layers of skin constituting the upper eyelids, and irises that are small in relation to the amount of white showing, but brightly sparkling. People with sheep eyes are prone to self-destructiveness and spells of melancholy.

3. Horse eyes are nearly triangular in shape, with heavily sagging upper eyelids and puffiness in the lower lids. They indicate a penchant for secret love affairs, a highly emotional person who is prone to accidents.

4. Wolf eyes are the "three-white-sided" eyes described earlier—the *sanpaku* ("three whites") condition in which the irises are small in relation to the eye, and the white of the eyeball shows below and to each side. Wolf eyes, however, are not a temporary condition but the eyes' permanent appearance; they are the sign of a temperament prone to cruelty and vindictiveness, a person who may resort to violence and unscrupulousness to get what he wants.

5. Monkey eyes are small in relation to the face, yet with large irises that show only a little white to each side; often there is a fold of skin at the lower eyelids. People with this eye-type are of an unstable nature, unpredictable and ill at ease in their home and work environments.

6. Hog eyes are of normal size but are distinguished by heavily lined or "broken" upper eyelids. They denote coarse or cruel instincts, a person who often finds himself in uncomfortable or dangerous situations.

7. Elephant eyes are long and narrow, similar to sheep eyes except that both the upper and lower eyelids are multiple folds of skin, and the eyes themselves rarely open wider than their normal size. People with elephant eyes are easygoing and affable, with the ability to approach even the most difficult problem calmly and solve it in a thoughtful, methodical manner.

8. Snake eyes are often called "*four*-white-sided eyes," since the relatively small irises appear as bright dots in a surrounding background of white. Like the snake, the snake-eyed person has remarkable patience but, when finally provoked, will attack violently.

9. Fish eyes have upper eyelids that droop at the outer corners, with a decidedly downward slant here as well. They are the sign of a nature that is as unstable and unpredictable as the eyes are placid and calm. The fish-eyed person often lacks vitality, may have difficulty interacting with others, but, paradoxically, usually leads a full and vigorous sex life.

10. Dragon eyes are perhaps one of the most desirable of the eye-shape types. They are large in proportion to the rest of the face, long in shape, with smooth, attractively tapered single eyelids that are almost always half-closed. The look of these eyes is sharp and powerful, possessing charisma and an air of authority; these, in fact, are the qualities of dragon-eyed people, among whom a number of great rulers and statesmen can be found.

The Eye Profile

The study of the profile is an important facet of physiognomy. Three general types of profiles are recognized in this study: the convex (curving outward), the plane (or vertical), and the concave (curving inward). Interestingly, the eye-type identified with each of these profiles indicates its owner's abilities as a talker.

The convex eye extends somewhat past the cheek, in keeping with the overall outward curve of this profile-type. Often the convex eye is noticeable because it bulges slightly. In general, this eye is the sign of a smooth, clever talker—a person who is self-assured in conversation, with an ad-lib answer for the most unexpected of arguments. This person is prompt at repartee, always ready with a quick and witty reply, even a succession of clever retorts. He can adroitly outtalk anyone, though sometimes at the cost of repetitiousness.

The plane eye combines the best features of the convex eye (above) and the concave eye (below). When viewed in relation to the normal cheekbone, the pupil of the plane eye is on the same vertical line. A person with this eye-type is also a good talker, but differs from the always-glib convex-eye person in that he must restrict himself to subjects with which he is completely familiar. When confronted with a conversation about an unfamiliar subject, the vertical-eye person naturally becomes a good listener. In these periods of silence he can weigh matters carefully and fairly, so that later, when he asserts himself, he becomes a convincing speaker, relying on firm conviction of his ideas. Vertical-eye people make excellent salespeople.

The concave eye is deep-set, with the pupil set back from the vertical line of the cheekbone. People with this eye-type are slow, careful talkers. If they cannot speak on a subject they know intimately, they remain silent. Like the vertical-eye person, the concave-eye person is convincing in speech, especially when he is allowed to continue for long periods of time.

Around the Eyes

Look for little giveaways *around* the eyes—the skin, lines, and moles that refine the reading.

Do the eyes seem especially far apart? Great width between the eyes signals a broad-minded nature, yet someone who will prove unmovable when he truly believes he is right.

Narrowness between the eyes, on the other hand, is the sign of a small or petty disposition, a person preoccupied with trifles, yet who will often rise to a strong sense of responsibility.

Check for vertical lines between the eyes. One line indicates a determined person who dislikes being distracted from his course. Two lines point to an entirely different sort of person—unpredictable and fickle, unable to focus on one project for long. Three lines are the sign of a down-to-earth optimist who enjoys life's simpler aspects and the satisfaction of simple tasks well done. Four or more lines are the mark of a multi-talented person with seemingly countless interests.

Many people have laugh lines or crow's feet, but whether they turn up or down makes a considerable difference. Upward lines point to a self-achiever, as well as to sexual indulgence and instability in love affairs. Downward lines indicate a sly person who finds romantic commitments difficult to honor.

A mole at the outer corner of the eye is the sign of a candid, direct nature, independent yet with a need for affection and respect to bolster a sometimes sagging ego. Over the right eyebrow, a mole signifies determination and a busy, successful life; over the left eyebrow, a tendency toward laziness and selfishness. And a mole embedded within the brow itself, right or left, indicates exceptional diplomatic skills.

The Eyebrows

Social success, emotionality, creativity, achievement— all are revealed in the shape, position, and texture of the eyebrows. But be careful! The eyebrows are perhaps our most frequently and dramatically altered feature, so that often we must read a "man-made" eyebrow not so much as an index to a person's character but as a key to the way that person *wants* to be perceived. Two famous examples are Joan Crawford, who wore strong, straight, prominent brows to suit her tough screen image, and

Greta Garbo, whose high, curving, pencil-thin brows bespoke that aristocratic unattainability which the studios felt made her so popular with movie-goers. What were the orignal shape and texture of these women's brows—and would their careers have been different had they retained them or shaped them differently?

In reading the eyebrows, begin by taking note of their overall appearance. Smooth, well-formed brows are the sign of a contented person in harmony with the world around him. Coarse, uneven brows, on the other hand, signify a person who tends to be lonely, his mind often in a state of turmoil or discontentment. Heavy or bushy brows indicate a strong, intense personality, one inclined to dominate and be unnecessarily blunt with others. Light or thin brows denote a fastidious nature, inclined to fussiness.

Now observe the brows' position in relation to each other and to the eyes. Wide-apart brows indicate a cooperative, adaptable person, but one who is too easily influenced by others. Close-together or "beetling" eyebrows signify an abundance of nervous energy; emotional outbursts are common. Do the brows ride high over the eyes? If so, they are the sign of a discriminating personality with uniformly high standards and the gift of diplomacy. Eyebrows that sit close to the eyes suggest affableness, a friendly, approachable personality.

Most important, take note of the brows' basic shape. Below is a list of the five most common eyebrow shapes.

1. Straight. An active, alert person who enjoys challenges wherever they arise—career, love, sports, and the outdoors. Intelligent, competent, and efficient, this is the organizer, a strong, level-headed individual who excels in any task except, ironically, the domestic variety. This is because he shuns the mundane, seeking beauty on higher levels—music, art, literature—and in the harmony of life itself.

2. Arched. "I see how thine eye would emulate the diamond," Shakespeare wrote; "thou hast the right arched beauty of the brow." Diamonds are appropriate here, for this is a person who enjoys the finer things of life. Success comes early and easily, yet this person perpetually seeks *more;* skilled at using imagination to turn ideas into practical steps of action, he is ruthless in pursuing goals. Though highly sexual in nature, and with a love of drama and romance, the arched-brow person enjoys stable, harmonious love affairs—and many of them! Perhaps this enjoyment is due to his ability to see a person's weaknesses and gently use this knowledge to dominate situations and relationships. Excitement and adventure are the key words here; creative, confident, and resourceful, this is the winner, the star, shining like—a diamond!

3. Rounded. An inquisitive person with shrewd ability in judging people's character and deducing their motives. Add self-confidence, resourcefulness, and a brilliant financial mind, and you have the consummate businessperson. On the personal front: a sharp, entertaining wit; a person who dominates in relationships both platonic and romantic.

4. Upswept. The ultimate go-getter—enterprising and aggressive, ruthlessly determined to reach specific goals. Words such as "no" or "impossible" do not exist for this person, always optimistic and positive, with a healthy pride and self-assurance that others find sexy. Whether his ambitions lie in business, politics, or the arts, this person is sure to realize them.

5. Downswept. These sad-looking brows denote their owner's desire for help in achieving his goals. Though he possesses innate imagination and foresight, he must make a concerted effort to take action, preferring to use sex or helplessness as a means of enlisting the aid of others. This person must guard against becoming the victim of those he depends on, ever strengthening his character against selfishness and a lack of resolve.

How long are the eyebrows? If short, they indicate general traits such as sexual passion and shortness of temper, an independent person with ambitions that change frequently. Short, thin eyebrows emphasize the loner, yet one whose sexual passion may turn into downright debauchery; this is a crafty individual who knows and, if necessary, will use less-than-scrupulous methods to get what he wants. Short, thick brows emphasize fickleness and instability; here is an aggressive trailblazer capable of overnight success, an ardent lover capable of sudden, explosive anger. In short, a person of great surprises.

Long, thin eyebrows denote the superior intellect of an artist or scholar; a serene, contented person who

Upswept brows are the sign of the ultimate go-getter—a person ruthlessly determined to achieve his or her goals.

dislikes sudden or radical change. If the brows are long and thick they signify a warm, dependable nature.

Other clues to watch for:

Brows joining over bridge of nose: determination and resourcefulness; a strong, straightforward nature.

Part of eyebrow runs in reverse direction: stubbornness, inflexibility.

Broken eyebrows (gaps or holes): treachery, deceit.

Thin outer tips bristling upward: generosity, bravery, resourceful ambition.

Double-curving (S-shaped) brows: artfulness.

Ledge across lower forehead, above brows: practicality.

Protuberances above brows, toward center of lower forehead: concern for detail.

Use this manual to make instant readings of your spouse, your lover, your family, friends, and coworkers, but keep in mind that physiognomy provides clues only to general personality traits. In the following chapters we'll explore the ways the eyes speak of our feelings and motivations in specific types of situations—beginning with the gazes and glances of affection and seduction in "The Eye Language of Love."

3

DRINK TO ME ONLY . . .

The Eye Language of Love

*For it is said by man expert
That the eye is the traitor of the heart.*

—Sir Thomas Wyatt, *That the Eye Bewrayeth*

The eyes those silent tongues of love.

—Miguel de Cervantes, *Don Quixote*

The Eye Pick-Up

Despite all his apparent smoothness, John was a young man suffering from a crisis of self-confidence. So when he set off for the office cocktail party that night, he figured a new conquest would be just the thing to shore up his failing sense of self. For John, eye language was a tool sharpened for a specific end. Let's see how he used it.

The party was in full swing when he arrived. He went immediately to the bar, asked for a whiskey and soda, and leaned against one of the stools, slowly swirling the ice in the glass.

His bright blue eyes began scanning the room, sizing up the crowd—the "prospects," as he would have said. The host and hostess were locked in animated conversation with a couple John knew from the office; he was sure he didn't want to become part of that circle. He noticed three middle-aged couples, married by the looks of them. Near the fireplace a woman stood alone, also surveying the crowd. John's eyes narrowed slightly, the upper and lower lids closing a little over the eyeball. No question about it, she was beautiful: tall, slim, wearing tight-fitting white pants and a loose peasant-blouse. Her ash-blond hair fell to her shoulders. She, too, had blue eyes, and after they'd finished weighing the crowd by the bar, they met John's gaze.

He waited, keeping his eyes fixed on hers; both their faces were totally expressionless. But just as abruptly her gaze moved on, and John, a little disappointed, continued with his own surveying.

At the end of the sofa sat a young woman with short, wavy brown hair and a pixieish face—not as beautiful as the tall blond, but pretty just the same. Her eyes met John's; again he waited. After holding John's gaze for no more than a second, she let her eyes travel down over his body. They lingered a fraction of a second and returned to his face. Now she smiled, her eyebrows rising and her eyes widening beneath them.

John returned her smile and very casually crossed the room to her. As he approached, her eyes remained fixed on his, but when he was about six feet away, she again let her gaze travel over his body. This time her smile was merely a turning up of the corners of her mouth, and her eyes were wider as they swept slowly down his body and remained just a little longer than usual there. John felt a tingling, for there was no mistaking her message. When she raised her eyes to meet his, she lifted one eyebrow and smiled. "Message received" was his answer.

"Hello," John said. "Can I get you a drink?"

"No, thanks," she answered, smiling up at him, and she took a cigarette from her purse. John responded instantly, holding out his lighter.

Her eyes were focused downward on her cigarette, but an instant later they lifted and looked at John openly. Her head was lowered coyly, but her eyes were boldly staring; there was no doubt about her message: "The eye game isn't the only one I'd like to play with you." By using this bold-but-submissive glance, she gave her consent, yet urged John on in the "chase" by seeming to back away from the encounter.

John sat down next to her and they began a conversation, but their eyes did most of the talking. Each held the other's gaze just a little longer than normal, exceeding the permitted "looking time" to test the other's intentions. Soon their gazes were virtually locked; the totally pleasant game of daring each other to look longer than normal was over. They had made up their minds. When their conversation had covered the usual cocktail party topics, John would again suggest a drink, and chances were good it wouldn't be in a crowded room.

Reading the Signs

Nearly everyone understands the eye language John sent and received. The body-glance, for instance—

focusing in on one's target—is one of the chief signals for expressing sexual desire. To glance at someone's body and let that person see the glance is one of the most provocative eye language signals we have.

To give someone the eye, put the eye on, give the glad eye to—all these describe a glance we know well, one as old as mankind itself. Shakespeare often referred to the powerful properties of this "come-hither" look. In *Othello,* Iago is attracted by Desdemona's seductive eye language: "What an eye she has! methinks it sounds a parley of provocation." And in *Romeo and Juliet,* Mercutio laments that Romeo has been "stabbed with a white wench's black eye."

In some Latin American countries, an ancient ritual called the *paseo* relies exclusively on the seductive power of this type of glance. Every Sunday, unattached young men and women assemble in the village square, with each sex forming a separate line. At a signal, they begin walking toward each other. If a man gives a woman the eye, or vice versa, and the recipient is interested, the couple may exchange a few words on the next walk across the square. Often this leads to a meeting and an equally stylized courtship.

But is the eye language of love always so easy? Sometimes our eyes can hamper rather than help our relationships.

Take, for example, an acutely shy man and woman who meet at a party and are drawn to each other. Immediately there is a conflict: Their mutual attraction urges them to look at each other, but their painful shyness will not allow them to do so. They seldom look into each other's eyes as they talk. Their gazes usually remain fixed on the floor or on some distant object, and though they may meet occasionally, these instances of accidental contact are brief and uncomfortable.

As they begin to feel more at ease with each other, their affection weakens the conflict between attraction and shyness. Their gazes meet more often now, but since there is still some uneasiness, one may give the other a longing sidelong glance—what we call "sheep's eyes" or, as Lord Byron wrote, "Stolen glances, sweeter for the theft."

"Long-looking"—or the lack of it—tells much about how we feel about someone, and is still the most trustworthy measure of a person's feelings. It's simply impossible to feign that special affectionate gaze that lovers give each other. "Her eyes never left his face," "He devoured her with his eyes," "He couldn't see enough of her"—all are everyday expressions that describe that look.

Of course, we all know people who try to imitate this long-looking signal to make someone *think* they like him. But this attempt usually turns into an overavid stare that is quite unpleasant and fools no one.

Meanwhile, back with our two shy young people, attraction is gaining the upper hand over shyness, and now they sit close together, gazing deeply into each other's eyes. Although they are totally relaxed in each other's company, with others they are still as shy as ever, and another relationship would take just as long to progress from floor-staring to deep gazes.

"Long-looking" is the most trustworthy indicator of how two people feel about each other.

Male Eyes vs. Female Eyes

Are the ways of eye seduction different for men than for women? Despite the feminists' insistence that men and women should enter sexual encounters as equals, the answer will always be yes. One of the sexes will always have the upper hand in eye seduction, and contrary to what you might expect, women are the dominators!

A good example is John's cocktail party encounter. Did you wonder why he didn't go for the beautiful blonde standing by the fireplace? John was experienced enough in the ways of eye seduction to know that if a woman doesn't signal sexual interest with her eyes—as the blonde did not—approaching her is a lost cause. He narrowed his eyes to try to concentrate his gaze, but when that was to no avail, he gave up the chase. Instead, he searched further and found someone whose eye signals were unmistakable. When her eyes met his and she smiled, he knew he'd found a partner for conversation. But when her eyes traveled over his body and lingered there, he knew they'd spend the night together.

If you don't believe the woman is the dominator in an eye pick-up, watch what happens at your next party. A man will rarely approach a woman and begin a conversation unless she's signaled interest with a second, sizing-up look; this is her way of granting him permission to speak to her. You'll be surprised at how few men will approach women who don't give this permission.

In settings where the atmosphere is not quite so conducive to romantic encounters—bars, for instance—not quite so much looking takes place. While at parties the woman is allowed a "free" meeting of glances with a man whether she follows up with a body-glance or not, in the bar that first glance is regarded as permission to approach her and strike up a conversation. If a man doesn't interest her, she simply won't meet his gaze at all.

So, however much a man may boast of his ability to pick up women, the women are actually the ones in control. Simply by deciding whether to look or not to look, they can screen the men to decide whom they would like to approach them. Traditionally, men have always had to play the active and women the passive role. The man was expected to approach the woman; it was considered shockingly forward for the woman to do anything but wait. But through the ages, women have learned to take advantage of their passive yet dominant position to control the situation.

Experiments have been performed to verify this pattern. In one test, fifteen male college students entered a room, one at a time, in which a woman was sitting. In almost every case, the woman and the student looked at each other once briefly as he entered, but no conversation took place unless the woman looked at the man a second time.

Men who are inexperienced in the ways of eye seduction will often pick the prettiest women to approach. These encounters usually result in a rude or disappointing encounter; naturally the batting average of these men is quite low. More experienced men like John—if they are considering nothing more than an immediate conquest—look for the women who signal their interest with a body-glance. Not surprisingly, these men's success rate is much higher.

But using the eyes to make contact with someone of the opposite sex is only the beginning. While we talk, the eyes continue to send out a variety of signals. Many women blink frequently while they're talking to a man they've just met. By itself, blinking wouldn't be very effective; the secret is the rapid movements of the eyes themselves.

Most women who have this mannerism are not even aware of it. Moving the eyes while blinking—or "batting" them, to use the old-fashioned expression—is a seductive tip-off in our society. Especially in the southern United States, this kind of flirting is almost a fine art; remember those Southern belles in *Gone With the Wind,* peeking delicately over their fans and blinking away when a handsome man came along?

Again, feminism notwithstanding, the eye language of love is different for men and women. If a woman bats her eyes as described above, most people think nothing of it—as long as it's not exaggerated. In fact, we're usually not even aware of it; it appeals to us on a subconscious level. But what would you think if a man you were speaking to began batting his eyes? Men do blink rapidly while listening intently during a conversation—as women do—but they tend to look straight ahead, and this makes all the difference. Long eyelashes have always been considered part of feminine beauty, and batting the eyes is a logical way to display them. We accept this mannerism as natural in a woman, but in a man it's socially unacceptable and calls his masculinity into question.

From early childhood, boys and girls begin adapting their own distinctive eye language. Boys are encouraged to be more assertive; they'll often look an angry parent or teacher straight in the eye. Girls, on the other hand, will often lower their eyes—a sign of submission, or of feigned submission, that will later become sexual in nature.

Beginning at puberty and sometimes earlier, men and women develop their own unconscious courting gestures, or gender signals. With men, these often involve clothing: straightening the tie, fingering the lapel, smoothing the crease in the pants. Women gesture with their bodies: tongue moistening lips, or hands smoothing hips. Then there are the eyes: long looks under seductively heavy, sleepy-looking lids, shy downward looks, and of course the wink. This last technique is probably the most contrived of our eye language signals. It is a teasing sign, a sign of sexual confidentiality, yet the actual act of closing one eye has no real connection to either of these messages. Or does it? Freud and Jung, primarily from their studies of the eye in patients' dreams, believed that these organs possessed sexual significance—in fact, that they symbolized the male and female genitalia. That the eyes can represent the testicles is shown in Sophocles' play in which Oedipus blinds himself for having committed incest; he has looked not only upon his naked parent—an ancient taboo—but also upon the results of his sin. The blinding thus becomes an act of symbolic self-castration.

If the eyes represent the genitals, then the blink might be considered a covering up in order to reveal— the frankest, yet most private, of sexual invitations.

In another play, a man, following a rapid courtship, asks a woman to marry him. Though she is pleased, she says she'll need time to think, since she's known him for so short a time. But the man wants an immediate answer, and suggests that she can find out easily whether she is attracted to him. He kisses the nape of her neck three or four times, and she reports the result (to the audience) by blinking rapidly, as if tasting something to decide whether or not she likes it. Opening and closing the eyes becomes a symbol for sexual consideration.

We even "blink" without blinking, for there are of course other ways of covering the eyes. The "peek-a-boo" hairdoo made famous by actress Veronica Lake, with the hair curving down to hide one eye, evoked in many men the desire to uncover and see the eye. Even dark glasses might be considered a form of blinking; we are attracted by an appealing face but want to get behind the glasses to read the sexual messages, if any, in the eyes themselves.

The Passing Look

A skillful glance doesn't run the same risk as a verbal proposition, yet it can be just as effective. Three fac-

We all know the meaning of this "come hither" look from under seductively heavy, sleepy-looking lids.

tors—length, direction, and intensity—determine the meaning a glance will have, and by varying the mix we get a whole range of subtle messages. For every social situation there is an accepted, or "moral," looking time. For two people passing in the street, the accepted looking time is only a second or two. When this glance is held longer, its meaning changes. With a smile or a nod it may mean "Don't I know you?" or "Haven't we met before?" Without the smile or the nod, the meaning changes again: "You look odd," or perhaps, "You appeal to me."

For centuries, men and women have made use of this principle in a technique we'll call the glance-and-look-back. A man passing a woman in the street may glance at her and lift one eyebrow ever so slightly, a gesture that both makes the statement "I find you attractive" and asks the question "Are you interested and available?"

If the woman is not interested, she will avert her glance and walk on. However, if her stride falters, if she stops to adjust her clothing or look into a store window, she is probably stating her reciprocal interest. When the man approaches her, eye language again comes into play. The length and direction of glances give both people important preliminary data on character, sincerity, and the degree of interest. Body language combines with eye language to supply a complete picture.

Eyes of Love

Once gazes and glances have helped two people find each other, the eyes are usually clear indicators that love has been kindled, even if one or both partners try to deny their feelings. An old song laments, "Your lips tell me no, but there's yes, yes in your eyes." Poets have praised the "heavenly" or "sweet, silent" rhetoric of lovers' eyes; in them we will find "love's tongue," "heart's letter," or "sweet music." As far back as the eighth century B.C., the Greek poet Hesiod described a man and woman from whose eyelids flowed "limb-unnerving love." Later, around the time of the birth of Christ, the Roman poet Ovid, considered an expert on the art of seduction, advised lovers: "Let your eyes gaze into hers; let the gazing be a confession. Often the silent glance brings more conviction than words." He advised women to keep their eyes "gentle and mild, soft for entreating of love. If he is looking at you, return his gaze and smile sweetly. . . . Love is allured by gentle eyes."

From the sixteenth through eighteenth centuries, a common expression was "to look babies in someone's eyes." "She clung about his neck, gave him ten kisses, toyed with his locks, looked babies in his eyes," wrote Thomas Heywood in *Love's Mistress*. Shelley described the same glance in *Prometheus Unbound*: "Think ye by gazing on each other's eyes to multiply your lovely selves?" Here, the eye is blessed with reproductive powers. The expression "to look babies in someone's eyes" is innocent-sounding yet at the same time quite explicit. Today, with our openness about sex, have we any expression that conveys this meaning in so few words?

"Bedroom eyes" describes the glance under lowered lids. By reducing the opened area of the eye, a person can concentrate his glance on an object or person in a more intense way. José Ortega y Gasset, the late Spanish philosopher, wrote of this look in his *Man and People*. The nearly closed lids, he said, shoot out the glance "like an arrow . . . It is the look of the eyes that are, as it were, asleep but which behind the cloud of sweet drowsiness are utterly awake. Anyone who has such a look possesses a treasure." The gaze of a painter who steps back from his canvas to examine his work in progress is an example of this lidded look.

The French call this look *les yeux en coulisse*—the sidelong glance. Madame DuBarry had bedroom eyes, as did the actor Lucien Guitry. Simone Signoret was famous for them, and many American actresses made this look their trademark—notably Clara Bow, Theda Bara, Gloria Swanson, Mae West, and Lauren Bacall. European men have used bedroom eyes to their advantage—Charles Boyer and Paul Henried are famous examples—and in America, Rudolph Valentino and Robert Mitchum were two actors who found that bedroom eyes can be as much of an asset in a man as in a woman.

Lovers' eyes are bright, and at one time people believed they actually glowed from a love-light burning softly behind them; lovers would even give each other miniature paintings of their eyes as tokens. "The light of the body is the eye," says the Book of Matthew, though it was Guillaume de Salluste du Bartas, a French poet of the 1500s, who gave us the best-known image of "these lovely lamps . . . these windows of the soul."

Les yeux en coulisse—the sidelong glance, made famous in Hollywood by sex symbols such as Mae West and Lauren Bacall. It's one of the most potent expressions in the eye language of seduction.

*   *   *

But the same eyes that can penetrate a lover's most intimate being can also signal the utmost respect for the rights and privacy of a stranger. In the following chapter we'll explore the ways in which we use our eyes to acknowledge and maintain other people's personal territories—the complex but unwritten set of rules that comprise the etiquette of staring.

4

SILENT INTRUSION

The Etiquette of Staring

*An eye can threaten like a loaded and levelled gun, or can insult
like hissing or kicking.*

—Ralph Waldo Emerson, *The Conduct of Life*

Eyes, you know, are the great intruders.

—Erving Goffman

What's in a Stare?

The rulebook of eye etiquette has always forbidden or
strictly regulated the stare. Our myths and legends re-
count tragic tales of people punished by the gods for
gazing too avidly or looking where they shouldn't have.
Even so much as a quick backward glance would bring
dire consequences, as in the case of Orpheus, who
turned back and lost his beloved Eurydice to the
Underworld; or of Lot's wife, who in her flight fom the
brimstone and fire that rained upon Sodom and
Gomorrah, looked back and became a pillar of salt.

We know from these stories of the past that the
stare was considered as great a transgression of accepted social behavior as it is today, if not more so.

"Peeping Tom" disobeyed a public edict by lifting his blinds and gazing lustfully upon Lady Godiva as she rode naked through the streets of Coventry to save her people from her husband's unfair taxation. His punishment, in the words of Tennyson: "His eyes . . . were shrivell'd into darkness in his head, and dropt before him." Another story tells of a woman who, curious as to how the saints passed their time, peeked into the cell of Saint Geneviève and was struck blind by God. And from an Arabian manuscript called *The Perfumed Garden* comes a warning that looking into a woman's vagina will permanently impair the transgressor's vision. Harsh penalties for a stare perhaps, but blindness has always been a common punishment for the eyes' misuse.

In today's society we teach our children that it's rude to stare—a lesson they absorb early on, perhaps because they sense that staring is actually far more than a simple matter of rudeness. They realize that the ways in which we instinctively look at others may express our true opinions of them—opinions we often would prefer not to disclose. Do we regard them as equals or superiors, deserving of our respect, or as inferiors? Do we consider them to be people at all? The basic rule behind what our parents taught us is that we simply do not stare at a fellow human being. We stare at *things*—paintings, buildings, scenery—and at animals, as long and as hard as we please. But when we stare at a person, we say with our eyes that we do not view him as a person at all, as someone with a "space" and privacy that we would no sooner arbitrarily invade than have our own invaded. On the contrary, we are treating him as we would an object or an animal—in short, as a nonentity. Needless to say, if we were to stare, whether out of curiosity or contempt, at everybody we felt superior to, the world would be full of constantly staring eyes, not to mention the fighting that staring would provoke, and at the least, the injured feelings. And so, because most of us would rather not hurt another person unnecessarily, we adopt the safer general practice of not staring at all—a practice that society has adopted as "polite."

Not surprisingly, there are exceptions to the rule—situations in which it's acceptable to stare, people it's acceptable to stare at. When we go to a fair, we pay to enter the sideshow and stare at the "freaks"—the fat lady, the man with no arms, the boy made of rubber. Here we've bought permission to stare at human beings as if they were objects. That the unfortunate people in the sideshow have been put on display in the first place tells us that society in general doesn't regard them as people at all. They are freaks or oddities, and no longer possess the right not to be stared at.

Many people have entered a sideshow once but wish never to repeat the experience, for they disapprove of putting human beings on display and pity the objects of this indignity. They cannot bring themselves to stare at other people as if they were objects. Perhaps they met the glance of a person in a sideshow and the unique, very human intimacy and recognition that can pass between two pairs of human eyes painfully reminded them of that person's "personness," made them feel ashamed for having regarded that person as a thing.

Another time we're expected to stare at others is when we go to see a play. As in the sideshow, we've paid for permission to stare, but here we feel comfortable watching the actors, primarily because they are not representing themselves. The roles they have assumed make them seem less like real people and more like objects *representing* people. Similarly, we feel no hesitation in staring at demonstrators, because they, too, *want* us to look at them. And at other times we'll stare not because we're expected to, but simply because others are staring along with us—at the scene of an accident, two people fighting, or the police arresting someone in the street. By withdrawing into the anonymity of a crowd we no longer hold ourselves responsible for our individual behavior, and feel almost as safe watching as if we were invisible or hiding. Our attitude is that it's all right to break the rules as long as no one knows we're breaking them; for what is a rule but something created for others to see us break?

In other social situations an individual is expected to stare at a large group. A lecturer, for example, can single out members of his audience and gaze at them— even make eye contact—for virtually as long as he pleases. Not only does the situation permit this type of eye behavior—indeed, the most effective speakers recommend it—but a second factor also comes into play. Experiments have shown that in large spaces such as auditoriums and lecture halls, where the viewing distances are greater and seemingly less personal, we feel an anonymity not unlike that of being in a crowd, and sense that it's permissible to look at people for longer periods than normal. This viewing period we have called the "moral" looking time, or how long it is acceptable to stare in any given situation.

Pass a stranger in the street, meet his eyes briefly, and look quickly away. You've stayed within the moral or acceptable looking time, and you've made the silent statement, "I respect you as a fellow human being and therefore will not stare at you." Hold his glance a little longer and you've gone beyond the moral looking time. The message is different now: "You look odd to me," or "Don't I know you?"; the stranger will probably stare back in discomfort, annoyance, or curiosity. Hold his gaze even longer and you may have a fight on your hands.

Eye-Threats and Eye-Cuts

We're all familiar with the power of a stare as a gesture of threat. Psychologists have even documented this power, as in an experiment in which motorcyclists and pedestrians purposely stared at car drivers stopped at red lights; when the light turned green, the drivers who were stared at moved off more quickly than those who weren't.

But how did the stare first become an invasion, a potential act of aggression and hostility? Biologists and psychologists agree that we react to more than the starer's simple act of watching us for an uncomfortably long period, and that glaring eyes threaten us most

The eye-threat, our most powerful expression of aggression.

strongly on the subconscious level. In fact, the threat we feel is an instinctive reaction built into many creatures as part of nature's survival system.

Low on the evolutionary scale is the group of animals whose coloring gives them the appearance of having extremely intense eyes, or even extra sets of them. Many species of butterfly and moth have spots that deflect birds' attacks from the insect's vulnerable body to its wings, or that even resemble the eyes of a larger animal staring out of the brush or the darkness. In some fish, eye spots expand during battle. And dark, menacing-looking eye rings help the raccoon establish dominance over its territory and repel predators. In each of these cases, nature was thoughtful enough not only to provide the animal with its trick eye-coloring, but also to build a fear of that eye-coloring into the animal's enemies. A vestige of this instinctive fear is still present in humans.

Primates (monkeys, apes, and human beings), the only creatures that consciously use their eyes to threaten, also *react* more strongly to a stare than any other creature. Monkeys and gorillas become angered and excited when other animals or men simply stare directly at them, and they respond with growls and threatening gestures. However, an equally common response to a stare—and not just among primates—is to lower the eyes as a sign of submission or weakness. A wolf will drop its eyes to acknowledge its leader's dominance, just as its relative the dog will often lower its eyes before its human master as a sign of affection and obedience.

Low on the evolutionary scale are creatures that nature has equipped with trick coloring that works on predators' instinctive fear of glaring eyes. For example: the owl butterfly, named for its owl-like spots.

As children we've all played the staring game, trying to prolong our gaze to show endurance and force the other to look away. As adults we play a similar game in more serious situations: the business meeting, where two individuals vying for dominance will engage in almost imperceptibly brief stare-downs; the family argument, where the member with the angriest, most piercing look may well prevail; the confrontation with authority, as when a policeman reasserts his power by fixing a steady gaze on and outstaring anyone who looks as if he might start trouble. Always the winner is the one with the longer, stronger stare, the loser the one who shows weakness by averting his gaze.

Because, as we mentioned earlier in this chapter, staring at someone often signals that we don't consider him worthy of respect, the stare of domination has evolved into an effective means of insult as well. We've already described the eye-insult in its most basic form: a rude, longer-than-acceptable stare says, "I do not regard you as a fellow human being, so I will not accord you human treatment." The eye-insult may also take the form of "cutting"— snubbing someone by looking at him with a bored, slightly unfocused look or a glazed, faraway expression. Here the message is, "Not only do I not regard you as a fellow human being, but you're not even an object: I don't see you at all!" "He looked right through me," a victim of this treatment might say.

Yet another form of eye-insult is the tilting back of the head and looking at someone through half-closed eyes—the gaze that gave rise to such expressions as "look down one's nose at," "turn up one's nose at," and "look down upon." Since the socially elite are said to hold their heads higher and tilted back farther than others, a person who gazes in this way signals that he considers himself superior to the person he's looking at. A servant, child, or criminal might receive this low-status look.

Polite Eyes

For the most part, however, we do our best to accord our fellow human beings the nonstaring status they deserve. We do so by following a set of unwritten rules that psychologists call "eye management."

A good example is the situation described earlier in which we're passing a stranger on the street. The first rule we observe is to acknowledge his presence, his fellow-humanness, by glancing at him only long enough to show him we've seen him, but then look away immediately. Now the second rule of eye management comes into play. As we pass, we signal our respect for the stranger as a person by deliberately not looking at him; a common practice is to set our gaze in the direction we're headed, or simply to look at the ground. Erving Goffman referred to this act of politely ignoring as "civil inattention," and has even verified that the point at which we feel compelled to implement it—when we feel we can no longer look at the stranger without "breaking the rules"—is when we are approximately eight feet apart.

Respect for another's privacy is a major factor in

these encounters, though sometimes our ability to extend this consideration is sorely tested. In England, for example, with its long history of overcrowding, the average citizen has developed an overriding desire for privacy. People passing in the streets of London rarely even make eye contact, as to do so would be to invade the other's much-valued "space."

The same holds true for most of the world's other densely populated areas. In New York City, people have had a reputation for being cold, unfriendly, or standoffish. The irony is that the New Yorker's "unfriendliness" actually comes from an almost sacred respect for the privacy of others; in most cases he would no sooner meet your eyes boldly on the street than stop and throw his arms around you. This overcompensation might be considered a vital survival technique, for without it, many of the inhabitants of this overcrowded city would find life unbearable. Can you imagine what New York would be like if its inhabitants felt as comfortable intruding upon other people's privacy—making eye contact, stopping to talk—as they might in a small village?

In general, a city's crowdedness makes the rules of eye etiquette difficult and sometimes impossible to follow. Eye management becomes a constant challenge. There are, for instance, people we must avoid looking at altogether in order to live safely and comfortably. We try not to stare at a panhandler, for if we were to make eye contact, we would open that all-important channel of communication—recognize and acknowledge his fellow humanness—which would in turn facilitate or even encourage his approaching us. Similarly, we avoid looking at someone who is passing out leaflets; if we meet his glance, he will try to hand us one. And, of course, we must never lock eyes with a stranger whom we discover staring at us intensely, for to do so would be to place ourselves in potential danger.

In cramped spaces such as subways, buses, or elevators, the moral looking time is reduced to virtually nothing, yet we're hard pressed to look anywhere without meeting someone's glance. As a solution, we've developed a whole set of ocular gymnastics to avoid giving anyone even the briefest of looks. We allow ourselves to glance briefly at the faces around us, but then our eyes must settle on some object—a coat, a shoulder, or, if we're lucky, a spare bit of wall. Often we unfocus our eyes as if we were hypnotized, seeing only a few inches in front of us. During the ride we may sneak looks at the people around us, but we must never meet anyone's gaze. If we do, we quickly look away to signal that the eye contact was an accident; sometimes we acknowledge this mutual understanding with a brief, impersonal smile.

We often use this apparently accidental look-and-away technique when we want to steal a glance at someone without actually seeming to stare, when too long a glance would cause embarrassment for either the viewer or the subject. When we see a celebrity or a severely handicapped person, we may look at him until his glance meets ours. Then it's our responsibility to quickly avert our gaze, as if we never intended to look in the first place.

Foreign Interpretations

Just as the rules of conversational eye behavior differ among various cultures, there are often drastic cross-cultural differences among the rules pertaining to the stare. In the United States, a man who wishes to be polite does not stare at a woman for any length of time unless she has signaled her permission with a gesture such as a smile or the lifting of an eyebrow. In France, on the other hand, it's acceptable for a man to examine a woman closely in the street, for this long-looking is interpreted as an expression of his admiration of the woman's beauty. Since Americans regard this type of staring as rude, many American women traveling in France become angry or embarassed when subjected to it—only to return to the United States, where the men don't stare, and feel suddenly less attractive!

Because such differences are often as tangible as language differences, people who must live and work in foreign cultures—diplomats, ambassadors, military personnel—find that they are most successful in their professional and private lives when they make an effort to learn these cultures' rules of eye etiquette, including those rules governing the stare.

Even within our own culture we expect some transgression of the rules of eye etiquette, for we realize that in any area of behavior a certain margin of transgression is virtually normal, contributing to the variety of human experience. But there are also extreme examples, such as the transfixed, soulless stare of the catatonic schizophrenic.

*   *   *

At the opposite extreme are the people who, usually out of some psychological need or disorder, seek not to prolong gazes and eye contact but to eliminate looking altogether. In the following chapter we'll analyze the gestures these people—and, unconsciously, all of us—use in an attempt to withdraw from the eye game: the eye cut-offs.

5

THE VITAL BLINK

Eye Cut-Offs

It is a basilisk unto mine eye,
Kills me to look on't.

—William Shakespeare, *Cymbeline*

If eyes don't see, heart doesn't break.

—Miguel de Cervantes, *Don Quixote*

A Delicate Balance

From the moment we awake to the moment we fall asleep, our day is a blend of input and output. We hear and speak; feel and touch; see and look—all in the proper equilibrium of receiving data or stimulus and sending it to others. In order to preserve good mental health, a person must maintain the correct balance of input and output to suit his particular psychological needs. If he does not, or cannot, maintain this correct balance, his mind's functioning will eventually begin to break down. Therefore, as part of his psychological survival mechanism, he makes use of a number of unconscious instincts—a stimulus thermostat, if you will—that decrease input and output as necessary.

When we are unnaturally deprived of the input and output that we receive from and give to other people—when we are alone too long, with no one to speak or listen to—we begin to crave these stimuli, or become lonely, and go out in search of human company. Laboratory experiments have documented this phenomenon more formally: people immersed in special fluid-filled isolation tanks that minimized their senses soon exhibited signs of psychological breakdown, and actually began to hallucinate in an effort to provide their own input artificially.

As harmful as too little stimulus is too much of it. A person subjected to more emotional strain (a form of stimulus) than he can handle may not only exhibit this strain through his personality, but may actually grow physically weak or ill. He may even suffer the combined psychological and physical trauma that psychologists call a nervous breakdown.

How do we maintain our perfect balance of input and output in this stimulus-filled world? The strategies by which we periodically restore this precious equilibrium vary almost as much as the individuals themselves—from vacations to meditation to quiet dinners with friends. Experiments show the danger of taking in too much input without countering it with these necessary recovery techniques. Sleep, for example, is one of our most vital means of restoring ourselves, the way in which our bodies reduce the mind's input virtually to zero after a long day of stimulus. People deprived of sleep for too long grow irritable and overemotional; their minds begin to have difficulty dealing healthily with input. Again, in a more formalized experiment, subjects who were repeatedly awakened every time they began to fall asleep soon showed signs of serious mental deterioration.

People who are unable to block out and/or recover from unwanted stimuli by natural means such as sleep may resort to artifical, and often harmful, ones. A classic example is the alcoholic, who "drowns his troubles (unwanted stimuli) in drink," or the drug addict, who takes a trip far away from the world (unwanted stimuli) by means of needles or pills. Unfortunately, these people are only temporarily numbing or blurring the stimuli rather than actually blocking them out or effectively balancing them; sooner or later the accumulated stimuli catch up with them, and they usually must seek professional help in dealing with this input in a new way.

The Blink as Cut-Off

One of our strongest sources of stimulus is vision, a signal the brain must constantly interpret and act upon. Perhaps it is *because* vision is our strongest signal that it is the only one of our senses that we can cut off immediately—simply by lowering our eyelids. Everyone has his own individual stress threshold, and the "cut-offs" we'll discuss later in this chapter tell us much about a person's stamina and vulnerability. But there is one cut-off we all indulge in regularly, thousands of times in a single day, and usually without even realizing it: the blink.

The blink is an eye-protecting reflex, distributing moisture over the cornea and removing irritants from the eye. It occurs in a fraction of a second, yet psychologists have concluded that it is far more than just a cleaning reflex, but also a meaningful mannerism or symptom—a form of cut-off.

When we blink, the eyeball rolls upward in its socket and certain workings of the brain are momentarily suspended. This "blackout" is, of course, so brief that we're not even aware of it, yet it's a rest the brain needs, a refreshing pause that allows it to recharge itself ever so slightly. As far back as the 1920s, scientists observed that blinking increases during anger and sudden excitement, suggesting its role as a relief or stimulus-blocking mechanism. In some people the blink may take the form of a tic that appears in states of tension and anxiety. Some researchers even insist that blinking is a form of "microsleep," and that too much blinking or microsleeping during the day may well be a cause of insomnia at night.

In addition to acting as a relief mechanism, blinking can provide the illusion of escaping the scrutiny of others. During that brief period in which our eyes are covered, we are "in the dark," unable to see our observer and therefore (our subconscious tells us) unable to be seen. Our reasons for wanting to "hide" may vary, but they usually stem from guilt or embarrassment, or from our fear of betraying ourselves in a deception. Evidence of this phenomenon is that many of us blink intentionally, in a rather sheepish way, to indicate that we're guilty of something; we're revealing our guilt by *pretending* we want to hide it.

Closing the Windows

Consider the number of times we close our eyes in the course of a normal day. We arrive at work, find ourselves deluged with various petty tasks, and, in a rare lull, close our eyes or cover them with our hands. Obviously, it's not our eyes that have received all the overstimulation; the office is full of sounds and even smells that assail us just as strongly as what we see. Yet it is not our ears or our noses we cover; it is our eyes. The reason is that, although our eyes may not *receive* all of the overstimulation, their signal to the brain is the most imperious. Closing or covering the eyes takes much of the pressure off the brain and provides relief from *all* the senses' stimulation.

Many doctors have recognized the benefits of this particular form of eye cut-off. Around the turn of the century, Dr. William H. Bates, a New York City ophthalmologist, based an entire program of relaxation and vision improvement on it—a program that draws thousands of followers to this day. Bates recognized that "overuse" of the eyes may cause physical and psychological stress, and invented a remedial exercise called "palming." Consisting of gently covering the eyes with the palms of the hands, palming derives the greatest possible benefit from a cut-off man has been using since he first appeared on earth. While the eyes relax in

Often in times of great emotional stress we must cover our eyes to block out stimuli we are temporarily unable to absorb.

the warmth and utter darkness of the cupped hands, they undergo a form of simulated sleep. The late British novelist Aldous Huxley, one of Bates's best-known followers, made these beliefs the subject of a book called *The Art of Seeing.*

Often we cover, or "screen," the eyes as a reflex action in sudden stressful situations, when our emotions must undergo great strain. We learn, for instance, that a loved one has died, or that another has miraculously survived an accident. By shutting our eyes we escape to the most private of all worlds—that within ourselves—cutting out unwanted stimuli so that we can better face the emotional impact of the news. If we did not take refuge by covering or closing our eyes, it is probable that we would momentarily cease to see anyway, since our mind must "dim" the other senses in its efforts to deal with this sudden input overload.

Fear and excitement are also causes of eye-screening. Whether we're watching a horror movie, shooting down the slope of a roller coaster, or driving our car straight into a collision, our first instinct is to shut our eyes tight. By refusing to see the inevitable, we subconsciously believe we can prevent it from happening. And, once again, in our excitement we are unable to accommodate so many types of sensory input at once, and so we eliminate the strongest, the visual.

If someone you know has a habit of closing his eyes frequently, consider it a clue that he's having trouble dealing with everyday stimuli in general. Whether or not he's aware of it (and most people aren't), he's try-

By refusing to look at something unacceptable, we subconsciously believe we can prevent it from happening.

ing to turn his back on the scene for short periods of time—and succeeding!

Watch for this type of eye cut-off and you'll learn much about people's ability to cope with life's everyday stresses and to "think on their feet." A mother surrounded by six children, all screaming at once for something different, might shut her eyes (oddly, she's just as likely to shut her eyes as cover her ears!) and virtually freeze, unable to function under such strain. Another woman in the same situation might simply stare staight ahead and methodically begin to deal with each demand. The first woman cannot cope, even with the visual stimulus removed; the second does not need to block out any input, and therefore has a higher stimulus threshold. Does her brain have a greater capacity for receiving, interpreting, and acting upon the countless stimuli of her environment? If so, is this an innate ability, or has she developed it like any acquired skill? Whatever the answer, eye-screening provides clues to a person's levels of intellectual resourcefulness and emotional stamina.

Inward Escape

Eye cut-offs in their most extreme forms are apparent in the mentally ill, demonstrating all too clearly these people's inability to deal with, or even receive, life's input. In a hospital or clinic one may encounter the chronic depressive who is habitually bent forward, his face hidden in his hands. This person is escaping the harshness of the world by blocking it out, withdrawing into the safe warm darkness of the mind. Sadly, he has adopted a gesture that is for most people a momentary refuge and turned it into a way of life.

Another extreme cut-off is the stare of the schizophrenic. His eyes are glassy and rolled slightly upward, with a faraway, remote gaze that seems to look right through people and things. His totally expressionless gaze shows no feelings—not because he *has* no feelings, but because he lacks the psychological connection necessary to focus them.

In simple terms, the schizophrenic sees but does not look—contrary to the popular belief that schizophrenics do not see their surroundings. Without actually lowering his eyelids, he has performed an effective eye cut-off and withdrawn from the world. He has fled in his own way, not by *blocking out* visual stimuli, but by not *interpreting and acting upon them* as they reach his brain.

According to the late Swiss animal psychologist Heini Hediger, every animal—including man—moves in an imaginary "bubble" that helps maintain proper spacing in relation to other individuals. "Personal distance" or "social distance" refer to the space between members of the same species during social encounters, while "flight distance" refers to the space between two individuals of different species at which one will turn and flee. An antelope will flee when an intruder is as much as five hundred yards away; the wall lizard's flight distance is only about six feet. At first glance, human beings would appear to have no flight distance, but it is present in schizophrenics, who often regard other people as intruders belonging to a foreign, and hostile, species. The schizophrenic flees not with his body but with his mind. When approached too closely, he escapes *into himself;* his flight distance is internal rather than external, and his eyes indicate this withdrawal with their glassy, "turned-off" expression. This type of cut-off is so indicative of schizophrenia that psychologists will often study a patient's eyes first to ascertain whether this illness is present.

Common Cut-Offs

Face-shielding and the schizophrenic's soulless gaze are the most extreme forms of eye cut-off, indicative of extreme psychological disorders. In our everyday lives we see milder forms of cut-off in practice—brief, subtle mannerisms many of us indulge in, most often unconsciously, to escape periodically from stress or input that we have difficulty assimilating.

In his book *Manwatching,* Desmond Morris discusses four specific types of this common eye cut-off. The first is the Evasive Eye, belonging to the person who rarely meets our gaze during a conversation. As we discussed in Chapter 1, we look away from our listener most of the time we're speaking. In this way we avoid unwanted input in order to get a better handle on what we're saying. We may also avoid meeting our listener's eyes if we're unsure of what we're saying, or if we feel shame or embarrassment. All these forms of gaze aversion are cut-offs, but normal, acceptable ones.

For some people, however, this gaze aversion is a

way of life; no matter how hard we try to catch their eye, they virtually never meet our gaze. Usually we attribute this Evasive Eye to shyness. What we're actually saying is that this person's self-esteem is so low, his insecurity so great, that he feels comfortable interacting with people only on the audio level, unable to bear the added intimate input that comes from another's glance. Because we rely so heavily on the eyes as indicators of emotions and intentions, we inevitably grow uncomfortable in the presence of someone with the Evasive Eye.

The second cut-off Morris describes is the Shifty Eye, belonging to the person whose eyes repeatedly dart away and then return to those of his conversational partner. This person is in slightly better psychological shape than the one with the Evasive Eye, for though he cuts off most of the eyes' communication, he does at least make periodic contact. Though he is psychologically better equipped to handle communication on a more intimate level, he is still not secure enough to accept the full range of the eyes' messages.

Similar in effect are the Stuttering Eye (the eyelids flicker up and down while their owner is speaking) and the Stammering Eye (the eyes blink but remain shut for abnormally long periods, as if having difficulty opening). Both these cut-offs block out much of the information the other person's gaze transmits, but, like the Shifty Eye, they do allow the eyes to gather some input from those of the other person.

How do we react to other people's unconscious eye cut-offs? Like stuttering in speech, the Evasive, Shifty, Stuttering, and Stammering eyes arouse a certain irrita-

We resort to gaze aversion in many stressful situations, when we feel comfortable communicating with another person solely on the audio level.

tion or annoyance in us, since they impede the smooth flow of communication. Subliminally we feel we're being blocked out, though in all other respects these people behave normally—a contradiction that makes the eye cut-off all the more confusing.

What we should keep in mind when we encounter an eye cut-off is that the person is not necessarily trying to block us out, but may be having trouble dealing with the world's input in general. The cut-off is his subconscious' way of finding a restful escape from the pressures and responsibilities of his life. By cutting down on his face-to-face interactions, he can more efficiently handle the day's overall input.

Eye cut-offs are a way of maintaining our mental equilibrium in a stress-filled world. Whether we put our hands over our eyes, shut them tight, or look away repeatedly during a conversation, we're performing a necessary psychological function, a withdrawal into the safest and most private of all worlds—that of our own minds.

Oddly enough, the eyes play a vital role in a survival technique that is diametrically opposite the eye cut-off: eye domination. Since he first appeared on earth, man has found it necessary to assert his will and his territory not only vocally but by means of facial expressions. The eyes played such a key role in focusing these expressions that very early, man began to endow them with powers beyond this world. In the following chapter we'll trace these powers—the "evil eye" from its primitive domination to the (barely) more civilized form we all employ today.

6

THE EVIL EYE—PAST AND PRESENT

Eye Domination Through the Ages

Thou tell'st me there is murder in mine eye:
'Tis pretty, sure, and very probable,
That eyes, that are the frail'st and softest things,
Who shut their coward gates on atomies,
Should be call'd tyrants, butchers, murderers!

—William Shakespeare, *As You Like It*

The silent upbraiding of the eye is the very poetry of reproach; it
speaks at once to the imagination.

—Clara Lucas Balfour

Early Evil Eyes

"If looks could kill. . . ." How often have we used this expression to describe someone's harsh or hate-filled glance? It is, of course, only an expression—a colorful figure of speech we use to comment on the eyes' communicative powers. But at one time people all over the world believed (and some still believe today) that looks *could* kill, and that this was only one of the many powers of the evil eye.

How far back can we trace this belief, and what are its origins?

Archaeologists have found cave drawings, dating from the third millenium B.C., in which large, glaring eyes feature prominently in the designs. The early ancient Egyptians were especially sensitive to the power of the eyes, and exalted their feeling to cosmic proportions. They saw the harsh Mediterranean sun as the relentless, burning eye of a malevolent spirit, who drank their water, parched their crops, and drained their energy. Later, the eye (or "iret"), symbolized by the sun, evolved into the Great Goddess, believed to have been produced out of (and still hold the form of) the High God, creator of the universe.

Several thousand years later, Shakespeare would incorporate this symbolism in his Thirty-Third Sonnet:

> Full many a glorious morning have I seen
> Flatter the mountain-tops with sovereign eye.

But to the Egyptians the great eye's aspect was sovereign in a terrible rather than flattering way. Its fire and blinding light came to be associated with emotions of similar magnitude, such as dangerous, unrelenting fury, which in turn evolved into a new symbol: an enraged, rearing cobra, believed to encircle the brows of the High God and shield him from his enemies. On earth this cobra appeared as the protector of the pharaoh's crown.

The eye appears again and again in the complex mythology of the ancient Egyptians, among whom amulets containing abstracted or stylized eyes became extremely popular. The sun/eye-of-god symbolism survives today as the eye that shines from atop the pyramid in the Great Seal of the United States. Representing God's eternal vision, the eye watches over us daily from the reverse side of the American one-dollar bill.

In the first century B.C., rabbinical scholars in the Holy Land debated as to what constituted the worst feature in a man. To Rabbi Eliezer it was an "evil eye"—an opinion seconded nearly four hundred years later by the Hebrew scholar Rab, who blamed the evil eye for ninety-nine out of every one hundred deaths.

"Eat not thou the bread of him that hath an evil eye," advises the Book of Proverbs, and Jesus declared, "If thine eye offend thee, pluck it out."

In medieval Europe, people with especially intense or venomous glances were suspected of being witches whose evil eyes enabled them to cause hiccups, headaches, exhaustion, accidents, sexual impotence, and sudden death with just a glance. Most of these people were executed automatically, for *The Witches' Hammerer (Malleus Maleficarum),* the infamous guidebook for witchhunters first published in Germany in 1486, warned that most witches, "by a mere look or glance from their eyes," could bewitch even their judges. Even as recently as 300 years ago, during the New England witch craze, "eyebiting" was held to be a very real and dangerous threat to the lives of God-fearing people, who could contract "the illness" when "overlooked."

The above are only a few examples of belief in the evil eye, a phenomenon that has occurred in virtually

The mythology of the powerful eye of God survives to this day, as in the eye watching over us daily from atop the pyramid on the reverse side of the American one-dollar bill.

every era and culture, and persists today. When John Roberts of the University of Pittsburgh examined 186 cultures throughout the world, he found that 67 of them still practiced some ritual connected with belief in the evil eye.

The Envious Eye

Jealousy, hatred, malice, contempt, hostility, astonishment, or exaggerated admiration—any of these envy-related emotions could accompany a glance and become the evil eye. The word "envy," in fact, is a combination and contraction of the Latin words for "to look" (*videre*) and "against" (*in*), also the root of the word "invidious." On the same etymological note, our modern word "ill" is a linguistic contraction of the "evil" eye that was thought to be the cause of poor health.

In many Mediterranean countries—Greece, for example—people often regard compliments as threats, since a compliment may conceal an expression of envy for another's possessions or good fortune. The deaths of babies and animals are sometimes attributed to someone's having admired them and given them the evil eye, and so mothers began to protect their children with all manner of spells and cradle ornaments to deflect the eye's deadly power.

Yet the complex of meanings connected with the evil eye goes beyond mere envy. Though we might be tempted to laugh at the importance of the evil eye and the rather fantastic cures and measures against it, this superstition grew out of universal human fears. The evil eye sprang from the power invested in a threatening or envious look, whether it was a momentary glance or a set gaze. It was seen as an assault or contamination in which its sometimes unwitting possessor had the ability to penetrate, by means of mysterious, invisible rays, people's bodies and souls at will, thereby influencing their condition or behavior. He or she took possession of the victim through the eyes—the spot where the soul was most vulnerable.

Beautiful children, talented people, pregnant women, and others experiencing unexpected good fortune are believed to be the principal targets of the envious evil eye. In the coastal villages of Tunisia, women stay in their houses as much as possible in order to avoid being admired. They dress their children in charms, amulets, and old, dirty clothes to keep from arousing the envy of childless women. Meanwhile, the male villagers, most of whom are weavers, deliberately limit the amount of work they do each day, so that supply does not exceed demand. Those who surpass the daily quotas are vulnerable to envy and, therefore, to the evil eye. Thus, in this instance, the evil eye serves as a form of economic control. Similarly, in India the fear of being envied puts some restraint on conspicuous consumption within a village.

Some people with especially intense gazes have been suspected of possessing the evil eye simply because they happened to be present at some tragic event, a kind of guilt by association common to superstition. Lord Byron was one. Another was Napoleon III, who had a piercing gaze under his heavy lids; a great believer in this phenomenon, he wore an amulet on his watch to combat his own evil eye. When crowds greeted Alfonso XIII, king of Spain, to Italy, they muttered *"mal occhio"* ("evil eye"), brushed their clothes to avoid contamination, and wildly rattled their keys to ward off the devil, known to fear both iron and noise.

How did one acquire the evil eye? The power was believed to be most commonly acquired through a pact with the devil, though in some cases this deadly ocular magic could be a curse visited upon the innocent—the "jettatore," who were said to cause misfortune everywhere they looked and to harm anyone who crossed their visual path. In Italy, successful, charismatic men were often believed to have the power. One was Pope Pius IX, elected in 1846, who was believed to be an innocent possessor, and whose benediction few requested; nearly everything he blessed turned out wrong, and many considered this blessing absolutely fatal. Once, during a procession through Rome, he glanced up at a nurse holding a child in an open window. The next instant she dropped the boy, who fell to the pavement and died.

In Guatemala the evil eye is considered to be unintentional: The wielder does not necessarily know that he possesses the power, and even if he does, he probably can't control it. Here, the usual victims are young children.

One of the most unusual beliefs as to how a person can acquire the power of the evil eye comes from Mexico, where a common folk concept is that *electricidad* (electricity) transmits *mal ojo* (evil eye)—an example of how the belief was able to survive and adapt to modern technology, which gave rise to an entirely new explanation for the ancient phenomenon.

Some have believed that everyone possesses the evil eye to some degree, and that it operates in a flash, so that the first glance of even an ordinary man, if tinged with envy or a related emotion, can send forth the malign influence.

Others insisted that it was passed from generation to generation—you could no more help having it than you could help having a hereditary disease. Some believed that the devil bestowed it as a gift to his most evil favorites, who could concentrate all their badness into their eyes and aim it at will. Yet others insisted that every eye contained a fiery substance that, like light through a magnifying glass, could be focused upon a person or object to cause destruction. And one of the most common explanations was that inside some people's eyes lived a malevolent spirit that could send out its destruction in the form of tiny invisible daggers. The expression "to look daggers at someone" is still used today.

Outstaring the Devil

There have been countless methods of combatting the effects of the evil eye—remedies, amulets, spells, and gestures—and even more ways of protecting oneself from being stricken in the first place. People wore cloves of garlic around their necks to repel the devil, sewed bags of bread and salt (or objects supposedly blessed by God) into their clothing, or stuffed these packages into their children's pockets before sending them off to school. If prevention was not successful, there was a variety of cures. In Greece, these rites involved oil, cloves, water, fire, and holy words; in the Middle East, salt, spitting, or burning alum; and in Ethiopia, breathing smoke or drinking holy water.

The most obvious way of outstaring the evil eye was to paint or affix eyes onto valued property such as buildings, ships, and even cattle, in order to ensure good fortune, a safe voyage, high productivity, and so on—a custom still practiced today. Many people have used symbols for eyes—bracelets, brooches, or bangles containing polished brass discs or smoothly buffed precious stones—that appeared to be simple ornaments but would presumably act as magical eyes to deflect the evil eye's power, turning it against itself. Sometimes a cord or chain was tied around the forehead and an amulet attached to hang directly between the eyes. In India, the forehead spot worn by women was probably originally intended also to deflect the evil eye, though it is usually worn for decoration today. Even knots and buckles were believed to have protective powers, for they not only approximated the human eye in shape (for deflection), but they also (in the case of knots) entangled the evil force and thereby kept it at bay. To this day, certain orders of nurses—for whom an occupational hazard is to come in constant contact with illness, the result of being "overlooked"—still wear these ostensibly decorative knots and buckles on their belts. Even the horse brasses now considered so quaintly decorative

Native Americans affixed the "God's Eye," made from sticks and dyed yarn or thread, to all manner of objects as a protective talisman against the evil eye.

were a protective measure: the discs of brass resembled the sun, renowned for its power to outshine the forces of darkness, and deflected at the same time.

Hand gestures originated as measures against suspected possessors of the evil eye. The most common was a fist with the small and index fingers extended—the *mano cornuta,* or "horned hand," symbolic of the devil and thought to be powerful enough to combat the magic of the devil's own horns. Today people wear plastic or metal good-luck charms representing the *mano cornuta;* a goat's horn; or, most popular among Italian-Americans, a chili pepper (as hot as the devil?). In the Near East, actual pairs of goat's horns are sometimes seen attached to the roofs of houses.

Latin Americans still make the "fig" gesture, or *feige,* by thrusting the thumb between the first and second fingers to represent the male genitals. The phallus is the most ancient and widespread symbol for combatting the evil eye. Men and women wore it in the form of amulets, hung these charms over the hearth, and even painted this symbol on doors and walls. The potent life-giving powers of this organ were thought to be "good magic" strong enough to combat the devil's worst. In ancient Roman times children wore a particular amulet called a *fascinum,* the Latin word for "penis"; the evil eye's spell-casting power was known as *fascinatio.* Both words were ancestors to our present-day "fascination," and expressed the evil eye's power to bewitch, or, in a manner of speaking, hold someone in spellbound fascination so that the evil magic could invade him through his eyes. In India, scarecrowlike dummies with exaggerated sexual organs are sometimes placed on the scaffolds of new buildings or in crop fields to repel the evil eye and ensure good fortune. And in Brazil, it was believed that a baby born making *the feige* would be blessed for life. The many babies who were not thus naturally endowed were given tiny, carved amulets representing hands making this sign.

Many of today's customs and everyday practices originated as measures against the evil eye. Jews still use a Yiddish-Hebrew verbal charm to keep away envious spirits while speaking of a happy event or an attractive child; complimentary remarks are quickly followed by *kayn ayn ha'rah,* or (contracted and slightly mispronounced) *kaynahorah*—"May there be no evil eye!"

Similarly, it was considered bad luck to boast of good fortune—health, wealth, happiness, or any other form—in any way, for to do so might arouse the envious evil spirits one had somehow escaped thus far. Beautiful children were therefore often disguised with ugly names or rags for clothing. Nor did one praise others, express admiration of them, or refer to *their* good fortune, which would be to endanger their happiness by drawing them to the attention of the evil eye. From this desire was born the traditional practice of understatement, or of negatively qualifying any compliments paid—a practice also common to the Japanese, and no more due to modesty or restraint than it is among the Jews. Those who were victimized by the unrestrained compliments of thoughtless or ill-meaning "friends"

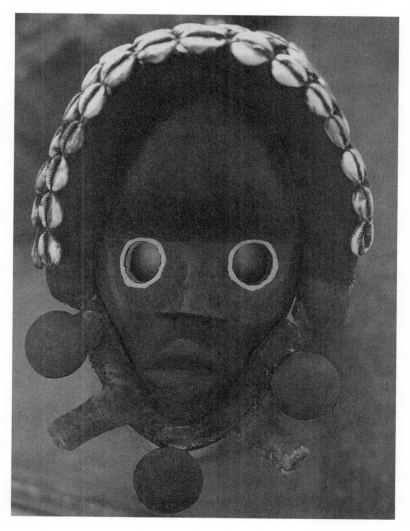

An obvious way of outstaring the evil eye was to affix especially large and frightening eyes to common objects such as this wooden tribal mask from Liberia.

would show no gratitude for the remarks, but would appeal to God as a bogey against the evil eye, thanking him for his blessing with words such as "hallelujah," once Hebrew for "glory be to God."

Yet another evil-eye countermeasure occurs at Jewish weddings, when at the very end of the ceremony the bridegroom crashes his foot down on a fine crystal glass. Both the sudden noise and the destruction of this valuable object are believed to divert the attention of the evil forces and prevent them from cursing the happiness experienced by the couple at that moment. This would also keep the potentially envious spirits from spoiling the newlyweds' future; as an additional measure it is traditional for the members of the congregation to shout *"Mazel tov!"*—"Good luck!"—as the glass breaks.

From the Orient comes the tradition of dressing a baby boy in blue or hanging blue balls or beads from his crib or carriage—a means of protecting the vulnerable infant from the malevolent glances of those jealous of his masculinity. Blue, divine color of the heavens, was known to be particularly distasteful to the devil. Thus, "blue for boys" began as far more than an innocuous custom, just as blue toys were far more than simply toys.

In some parts of Europe, people still spit three times at anyone thought to have the evil eye, since human spittle was once regarded as a holy substance, a product of man's soul. In the same vein, spitting once over one's shoulder is believed to be a way of catching the demonic eye unaware and blinding it. And women in the Middle Ages would rub their spittle on their babies' foreheads, hoping to build a permanent immunity in them.

It was possible to possess the evil eye even in death. Some ancient peoples closed the eyes of the dead and placed weights on their lids so that the spirit haunting the body could not cast its evil eye upon the living. An old superstition among the Amish in Pennsylvania says that if the eyes of a corpse are left open, another person will die, because the evil eye within the corpse is looking for someone to kill.

Through the ages, man has invested the eyes with extraordinary, fearful powers. The Cyclopes, ferocious giants with one eye in the center of their foreheads, were mythological symbols for death and destruction. At the other end of the spectrum, Argus Panoptes, who had one hundred eyes, was represented as the devil. Cross-eyed people and those who squint have also been considered bad luck, as have people who are unfortunate enough to possess an eye color uncommon to their geographical region.

Like magic and witchcraft, the evil eye has provided an explanation for random events that are otherwise inexplicable—from mental illness to disease, to disaster, crisis, famine, and death. Whether the evil eye is superstition or fact, people throughout the world have been so strongly influenced by the eyes' power to convey negative emotions that they believed these organs could cause physical harm.

The Dominant Eye

Today, evil-eye superstitions are rare in western cultures, vestiges of a simpler past. But the force behind these superstitions—the threatening power of the eyes—will always be with us. We all encounter eye-threat situations in our daily lives, and though these ocular messages may take a subtler and more civilized form, they are as effective as they ever were, domination techniques that draw their power from our primal fear of an intense look. These techniques might well be called the modern-day evil eye.

Let's take one of the most commonly used of these modern-day eye-threat techniques: the dominant-subordinate gaze. Most commonly, one person holds power over another by virtue of his elevated social or hierarchical position. This dominator may be a military officer, a policeman, an employer, a teacher, or a parent. By glaring intently at a subordinate—a soldier, a traffic violator, an employee, a student, or a child—he or she works on the subordinate's feelings of inferiority or guilt and forces him or her to look away in embarassment or to signal obedience. Literally, the subordinate is "losing face." Our society's eye-language conventions dictate not only that the subordinate must avert his gaze under the glare of a dominator, but also that the dominator may regulate *where* the subordinate must look. For example, a soldier is not permitted to meet the gaze of a reprimanding officer, but must stare straight ahead, keeping his facial expression as impassive as possible. And an unwritten rule says that a child

We have all encountered the dominating eye-threat, a modern version of the evil eye.

who is being scolded by a teacher must look downward as a sign of respect.

In our daily lives we encounter numerous situations in which eye-domination plays a key role. A policeman, for example, will often use a form of eye-threat in the performance of his duties. When he stops a speeding driver, he will stand beside the driver's window and glare down at him, taking advantage of both his own elevated position and the driver's innate fear of authority.

The airport customs agent uses a related form of eye-domination to help him in his job. When we step up to his inspection station and hand him our filled-out declaration cards, he looks first not at the card, but directly into our eyes. Though he may be smiling, subconsciously we feel the intended warning of his gaze: "Look me in the eye," it challenges us, "or I must assume you're trying to hide something."

Most often it is the travelers who avert their eyes who are asked to open their bags. Because most of us know or instinctly sense this, we look the inspector directly in the eye in order to declare our honesty and thus avoid being held up for inspection—even when we have nothing to hide! When we *do* have something to hide, we make a special point of meeting his gaze to give the illusion of honesty and a clear conscience. Though this sometimes works, a truly skilled inspector can usually recognize an overzealous gaze—a falsification of our eye language—and will ask us to open our bags.

As we saw in the case of the policeman looming

above the traffic violator, a factor other than actual authority can play a role in the dominant-subordinate gaze. Edward T. Hall, in *The Hidden Dimension,* calls this factor "social distance," a central element in his science of space relationships, proxemics. The type of social distance at work in both the teacher-student and policeman-driver situation is the close phase, in which the two participants in an encounter are from three to seven feet apart. Hall describes this as "the distance at which most people carry on impersonal business—people who work together, or are attending a social gathering. When two people are speaking at this distance, there is a domineering effect . . ." The dominator's higher physical position renders his gaze all the more effective.

Most of us are instinctively aware of the psychology of physical position—an awareness that causes us to rise to our feet to confront an oncoming antagonist, or get out of our car as the policeman who has stopped us approaches. Despite our official relationship to our opponent, our first instinct is to try to equalize the situation.

One often finds the dominant-subordinate gaze combined with social distance in business situations. For example, an executive talking to his secretary or receptionist will often reassert his higher status by standing in the close phase and staring down. On the other hand, the same executive might speak to visitors in the far phase of social distance—seven to twelve feet— which is most effective in situations where two people in an intrinsically adversarial relationship (negotiators, for instance) must keep up a pretense of being allies. The sheer size of the executive's desk usually guarantees

that this distance will be maintained. Often the dominator will strengthen his position by ensuring that his
visitor's chair sits lower to the floor than his own.

Today an increasing number of business people
are doing away with the traditional massive desk in
favor of loungelike areas containing chairs or couches
on which they can hold more casual discussions with visitors. These executives realize that being dominated
makes most people feel ill at ease—a definite disadvantage in most business situations—and therefore choose
to equalize encounters through eye language and proxemics.

The Manipulative Eye

Not all of the eye-threat situations we experience in our
daily lives follow patterns as relatively simple as that of
the dominant-subordinate gaze. Consider, for example,
the rather common encounter between a salesman and
his prospective buyer. Because our natural instinct is to
hold onto our money, and the salesman's purpose is to
arouse emotions in us that will overpower this instinct
and cause us to buy, we sense a threat or invasion when
he approaches, and steel ourselves to resist his efforts.

One might at first imagine this to be one more example of the dominant-subordinate gaze, with the wary
customer doing the threatening or dominating. What
makes the situation far more complex, however, is that
if the salesman is to make his sale, *he* must become the
dominator, yet give the impression of being the subordinate. The salesman knows from experience that the

Two strikingly opposite eye gestures. The woman on the left strikes an ingratiating, almost coquettish pose, combining a smile with the kind of sidelong glance usually used seductively. The woman on the right tries to assert social dominance by "looking down her nose" at us, a way of creating social distance.

feeling of being dominated, of falling under the salesman's power and being swayed by his pitch—the same fear that made the customer resist in the first place—is what frightens off many a would-be buyer. He must therefore use his selling skills and body language to walk that very thin line between persuasion and domination, allowing the customer to feel he's continuing to dominate through his initial resistance to buying.

How does the salesman dominate—yet not dominate—through eye language?

First, to win the prospective customer to his side, he conveys sincerity and confidentiality by purposely making frequent eye contact, knowing that this direct looking will be unconsciously interpreted as a sign of honesty. However, in order not to seem to dominate or threaten, the salesman is careful not to glare or stare too hard, and to complement his eye language with facial expressions such as a solemn lowering of the eyebrows or a broad smile—further signs of honesty and fellowship that have a subconscious favorable effect on the prospective customer.

Second, the salesman carefully observes his target's eye signals in order to gauge how the sale is going—or not going—and how best to proceed. For example, eyes that have begun to wander indicate a loss of interest; the salesman will take his cue and suddenly do something unexpected, such as a startling demonstration, a revelation of one of his product's hidden uses or applications. On the other hand, eyes that are downcast or look sharply away tell the salesman that his prospect is shutting him out in defiance. The salesman realizes that he has probably been selling too hard, and that if he continues in this manner his chances of a sale are remote. He therefore must stop and try to salvage the situation by rethinking his approach in order to suit this particular customer. An inoffensive soft-sell is probably best here.

The salesman will know his pitch is having its desired effect when the prospect's eyes frankly meet his own, with a deliberate blink now and again, and the brows slightly lowered—signs of serious consideration. If the blinking becomes more rapid, the eyes shifting thoughtfully away for brief periods, then the consideration has progressed to the point where the prospect is imagining himself owning and using the product; the salesman knows it's just a matter of time. Finally the prospect looks the salesman straight in the eye, the lids lowered in a relaxed manner, and says those all-important words: "I'll take it!"

As we've seen, eye domination today takes a number of diverse forms—from the vestigial evil eye still believed in by many cultures around the world, to the authoritative glare of an employer, parent, or teacher, to the sending and receiving of subtle eye signals that cleverly manipulate a rival or colleague. Whatever the form, eye-domination is a large and important part of the eyes' language, arousing in us instinctive responses that can be tracked back to the psychological behavior of our ancestral cave-dwellers. Watch closely the eye language of those around you, making note of how they dominate and manipulate. Though you may not choose to make use of these techniques yourself—consciously, at least—you will be able to recognize eye-domination in others and make an effort to resist.

Once again, an understanding of the eyes' signals and how they affect us can be the key to richer, freer lives. This understanding can even include signals that will tell us everything from how much our lover really cares to whether we are suffering from a serious degenerative disease. These are messages sent out by the purely *physical* eye; specifically, the pupil and the iris— the sciences of pupillometry and iridology, whose secrets we will explore in Chapter 7.

7

SECRETS OF THE INNER EYE

Pupillometry and Iridology

Listen to a man's words and look at the pupil of his eye. How can a man conceal his character?

—Mencius

He kept him as the apple of his eye.

—Deuteronomy 32:10

Man in Miniature

Thus far we've seen how our glances reveal our emotions and character, as well as how the movements of the skin around our eyes combines with these glances to send out an additional variety of messages. Except for the discussions of the physical eye in Chapter 2, we have dealt primarily with eye *interaction*.

But within the eye itself—the physiological eye—further revealing secrets may be read. Our pupils, for instance, are one of the most accurate gauges of our true likes and dislikes in virtually any area.

The pupils are openings that admit light into the eyes, narrowing and enlarging automatically as the amount of light falling upon them increases and decreases. In the brightest light they can narrow to tiny black dots measuring only two millimeters across. In utter darkness they can widen to as much as four times this size.

Other factors cause change in pupil size. When we focus on close objects, our pupils become smaller as the lenses adjust to a shorter viewing distance. Pain, loud noise, and certain drugs that have been introduced into the bloodstream or placed directly in the eye cause our pupils to dilate or contract. Certain diseases may also cause either dilation or contraction. And brain damage may be indicated by a difference between the size of a person's two pupils; the exact amount of difference can even help the doctor to locate the damaged area.

But what few realize is that most of the pupils' size changes are due not to causes such as the above but to our intellectual processes, our thoughts and emotions. The late psychologist Eckhard Hess wrote that "Embryologically and anatomically, the eye is an extension of the brain; it is almost as though a portion of the brain were in plain sight for the psychologist to peer at." Pupil constriction and dilation are performed by the eyes' radial dilator muscles, which are in turn controlled by the body's sympathetic nervous system. Thus, when we feel an emotion such as fright, our pupil response is akin to other involuntary reactions within the body: increased heart rate, higher blood pressure, quicker breathing, more profuse sweating.

Psychologists have made accurate recordings of pupil responses to subtle emotions and types of mental activity by having subjects view stimuli—slides of objects, places, and the like—in an optical box equipped with a camera that can film the eyes as the pictures come into view. This optical box is the most reliable recording method because it ensures that the amount of light to which the eyes are exposed is constant; experimenters can be certain that the pupils' size changes are due only to the emotional impact of the pictures being viewed.

What basic patterns do our pupil responses follow? Very simply, our pupils dilate when we see or experience something interesting, pleasant, appealing, or exciting, and they contract at something distasteful, unappealing, or repellent. What makes these mood cues so psychologically valuable is that they are basic, innate reflexes, occurring without our even being aware of them. Though it is possible to fake some glances, pupil reactions are totally beyond our control, and are therefore amazingly accurate gauges of our pleasures and fears, likes and dislikes.

People in past times recognized that pupil size-changes held some significance, though they never understood exactly what these cues indicated, or what caused them. In their poetry they speak of eyes growing "large with love," as "wide as saucers," or as "pinpoints of hatred." The expression "the apple of one's eye" originated in the ninth century, when the Anglo-Saxon word "aeppel" meant both "apple" and "eye." When a person's pupils dilated with affection, the image of the person filling each pupil became, figuratively, the apple (or the eye) of his eye. In an even earlier time, this image was believed to be a precious little doll that in-habited the pupil, a word that comes from the Latin *pupilla:* "tiny doll," the diminutive of *pupa,* or girl. The Hebrews, on the other hand, called the pupil *eeshon*—"a little man."

People knew that one's pupils dilated when he or she was experiencing sexual arousal. A story tells of Casanova, one of the greatest lovers of all time, spend-ing four hours in bed with a woman who afterward complained of hunger and demanded that they join a dinner party. Casanova warned her that the size of her pupils would be a sure giveaway of what she'd been up to, but she insisted nevertheless, saying that she knew this was true, and wanted to make all the other women at the party jealous of her ultimate conquest. Similarly, in *The Psychology of Marriage* Balzac advises men that if their wives are thinking of taking a lover, the men can read these wanton desires in the women's eyes because their pupils will become darker—a reference to their growing in size.

People to whom it is important to know what someone else is thinking have made use of pupil-size cues to varying degrees for quite some time. For exam-ple, jade dealers in pre-revolutionary China, aware that their pupils grew larger when their interest was aroused by an especially valuable gem, not only wore dark glasses so that customers they were trying to cheat would not become suspicious, but they also watched for dilation in their customers' pupils—an almost certain sign that they had spotted something they liked well enough to pay a handsome price. Turkish rug merchants used this latter techique to sell inferior merchandise to naïve European tourists, and some magicians, while doing card tricks, can identify the card a person is thinking about by watching for pupil dilation when the card is turned up.

Eye Appeal

Over the past thirty years, scientists have used the optical box to record subjects' reactions to various sets of pictures. In one of the earliest of these experiments, a picture of a baby was shown to three groups: single men and women; married men and women *without* children; and married men and women *with* children. The women in all three groups, whether married or single, with or without children, showed dilation, a pleasurable response. However, only those men who had children of their own showed similar dilation; the childless men, whether single or married, showed constriction, a negative response. Bearing in mind that this experiment was conducted nearly fifty years ago—at the height of the baby boom—we can see reflected in the women's responses the generally accepted attitude that children were one of the most desirable of a woman's occupations. It is safe to assume that if this experiment were performed today, the women's response would not be quite so uniform, and would probably align far more closely with the responses of the men.

One of the first experimenters with pupil size-changes was Eckhard Hess, who began his study of what he called "pupillometrics" while head of the psychology department at the University of Chicago. In an article in the April 1965 issue of *Scientific American* entitled "Attitude and Pupil Size," he begins by describing the incident that led to his investigations:

> One night about five years ago I was lying in bed leafing through a book of strikingly beautiful animal photographs. My wife happened to glance over at me and remarked that the light must be bad—my pupils were unusually large. It seemed to me that there was plenty of light coming from the bedside lamp and I said so, but she insisted that my pupils were dilated. As a psychologist who is interested in visual perception, I was puzzled by this little episode. Later, as I was trying to go to sleep, I recalled that someone had once reported a correlation between a person's pupil size and his emotional response to certain aspects of his environment. In this case it was difficult to see an emotional component. It seemed more a matter of intellectual interest, and no increase in pupil size had been reported for that.
>
> The next morning I went to my laboratory at the University of Chicago. As soon as I got there I collected a number of pictures—all landscapes except for one seminude "pinup." When my assistant, James M. Polt, came in, I made him the subject of a quick experiment. I shuffled the pictures and, holding them above my eyes where I could not see them, showed them to Polt one at a time and watched his eyes as he looked at them. When I displayed the seventh picture, I noted a distinct increase in the size of his pupils; I checked the picture, and of course it was the pinup he had been looking at. Polt and I then embarked on an investiga-

tion of the relation between pupil size and mental activity.

Subsequent experiments have recorded sexual responses by having subjects view pictures of clothed and unclothed men and women in the optical box. One of the first results of these tests was proof that, contrary to popular belief, women find naked bodies just as exciting as men do. Predictably, heterosexuals dilated more to nudes of the opposite sex than to nudes of their own sex, while in homosexuals the results were the opposite.

These pupil tests can also reveal subjects' true social attitudes and prejudices. In one experiment a picture was shown in which a black man and a white woman were kissing. When questioned before the test as to their views on racial equality and integration, all of the subjects registered total approval. However, only half the group showed dilation or no change in pupil size; the other half showed extreme constriction. The test had weeded out the pseudo-liberals from the real ones.

Even pictures of food have been tested for pupil response. Hungry people showed more dilation to pictures of food than did people who had just eaten. Others were asked what foods they liked and disliked, then shown pictures of the ones they had named. In nearly all cases dilation correlated perfectly with stated preferences. However, in a few cases subjects' pupils did not constrict (indeed, they often dilated) at pictures of foods they had said they disliked. Eventually the reason for this inconsistency became clear: these people were dieters, and had convinced themselves—outwardly, at least—that they no longer liked forbidden foods. But as their pupil responses revealed, subconsciously they still craved them.

Eye to Eye

More recent tests have shown that our pupils dilate not only to pleasurable stimuli, but also at the sight of other people's dilated pupils! In one of his best-known experiments, Eckhard Hess showed a group of men two sets of the same pictures of pretty young women. Hess had had the photographs carefully retouched, so that in one set the women's pupils were very small, and in the other they were very large. The men were asked to study the pictures and describe what they imagined the women's personalities to be like. The faces with the enlarged pupils were rated "soft," "pretty," and "feminine," while those with the small pupils were considered "hard," "selfish," and "cold." Though the men felt these reactions strongly, not one could explain *why* he felt the way he did—proving that the effect pupil size has on our reaction to others is purely subliminal.

What had happened in this experiment is that the women's dilated pupils were a nonverbal sign of sexual stimulation to the men, who, sensing that the women found them appealing, also became stimulated and dilated as well! The results of this mutual signaling were even more dramatic when the women had blue, gray, or green eyes, the reason being that the lighter the irises, the more apparent the pupils and their dilation. Could

The lighter the irises, the more apparent the pupils and their dilation—a sign of pleasure. Is this why so many people find light-eyed people so attractive?

this be one reason why many people find light eyes so sexy, and black eyes, which often seem to be all large, dilated pupils, so romantically beautiful?

The courtesans of Renaissance Italy were aware of the alluring properties of dilated pupils, and consciously manipulated this signal by dropping into their eyes a drug distilled from the deadly nightshade plant. Because these women knew that the drug made them more appealing, it took on the name of belladonna— "beautiful lady." Today this manipulation is carried on not by courtesans but by the most sophisticated advertising agencies, and not with belladonna but by the method Hess used in his early experiments: retouching the eyes of people in photographs to make their pupils appear dilated. In our daily lives we often make use of the dilated pupils' messages without even realizing it— simply by turning the light down low for romantic or intimate occasions. Not only is dim light or candlelight physically flattering, but our pupils, expanding to compensate, also work subliminally to make us all seem more attractive to each other.

But dilated pupils do not always have this arousing effect. One group whose pupil responses were tested consisted of avowed male "swingers," who enjoyed sexual relations with women but refused to form any sort of permanent attachments. These men did not show the average amount of dilation to pictures of beautiful women, yet when they viewed pictures of women with constricted pupils, their own pupils dilated! In other words, they were cautious of women with normal or dilated pupils, which they subconsciously associated with a desire for lasting relationships. Women with constricted pupils—a sign that they were experiencing less emotion and therefore seemed not to desire any sort of real love relationship—were appealing because they presented no such danger. Interestingly, homosexual men also preferred women with constricted pupils, for these men possessed the same fear of women who posed any sort of emotional or sexual threat.

The Body Screen

While our pupils reveal our likes and dislikes, the irises surrounding them serve as gauges of our overall health.

The study of the iris as an index to the state of the body is by no means a recent development. The civilizations of Mesopotamia and the Indus Valley watched the eyes for the first signs of disease, as did the Greeks, the Babylonians, and the Chinese, who for centuries have included an examination of the eyes in any routine diagnostic procedure. The Native Americans of the southwestern United States developed the related art of sclerology, the reading of health from the tiny blood vessels in the whites of the eyes.

Modern medicine has long recognized that certain disorders within the body are revealed in the eye. For example, the conjunctiva (the mucous membrane lining the inner eyelids) adopts a bright yellow tint in cases of jaundice, and becomes inflamed during measles or scarlet fever. Vitamin deficiencies are often indicated first by a waxy reddish look over the entire eye.

Recurring attacks of blindness may precede the affliction of multiple sclerosis by several years, while sudden blindness in one eye may be a sign of arteriosclerosis, cardiac disease, diabetes, nephritis, septic infection, or uremia during pregnancy. Night blindness may be caused by vitamin shortages; blindness in the outer halves of the field of vision, by an enlarged and possibly tumorous pituitary gland. And general loss of sight may signify malaria; poisoning from arsenic, lead, quinine, or wood alcohol; or, when vision dims and a dark cloud seems to appear directly before the eyes, an amblyopia caused by tobacco or alcohol.

It is not surprising, then, that the iris should prove to be one of the most faithful monitors of the status of every organ of the body. The origins of this particular science date back approximately two hundred years, when a young boy in Hungary made an unusual observation.

In the early 1800s, eleven-year-old Ignatz von Peczely, a native of Egernar, near Budapest, caught an owl one day and struggled with the bird as it tried to use its sharp talons to free itself. Von Peczely accidentally broke the owl's leg, and immediately noticed a thin black line forming in the upper portion of each of its irises. Though the boy bandaged the leg and nursed the owl back to health, finally giving it its freedom, the bird remained in the garden for several years, and von Peczely had an opportunity to watch further changes that took place in its irises. As the owl's leg healed, the black line was replaced by crooked white lines, which eventually became a tiny black spot surrounded by white lines and shading.

Von Peczely grew up to become a physician, and never forgot what he had seen in the eyes of the owl. While working in the surgical wards of Budapest's college hospital, he observed the irises of accident patients before and after surgery, and, as in the owl, saw a definite correspondence between conditions in various parts of the body and markings in certain areas of the iris. Like the owl, people with broken legs showed lines in a particular portion of the iris; those with heart trouble had a certain diamond-shaped mark. From his findings, von Peczely created the first iris-reading charts, wrote a treatise in 1868, and published a book in 1880.

Meanwhile, a Swedish minister named Nils Liljequist independently discovered a relationship between the settlement of various chemicals and drugs in the body and specific discolorations in the iris. Extremely ill as a youth, Liljequist had taken massive doses of quinine and noticed a yellowish-green discoloration in his irises. In 1871, he, too, published a book on his findings.

From these two pioneer works came the art of iridology that has been practiced in its modern form for decades by German physicians and is steadily gaining popularity throughout the world.

A Natural Reflex

Iridology, a facet of the holistic health movement, is based on the premise that the body is a marriage of its individual parts, and that a disorder in one part of the body is often reflected in another. In this case, each organ of the body corresponds to an area of the iris, so that when an organ malfunctions, it is reflected in the eye.

What makes this eye-body correspondence possible is that the approximately one-half million nerve filaments in the iris are closely tied in with the cervical ganglia of the sympathetic nervous system—part of the autonomic nervous system, which regulates the functions of the heart, intestines, and glands. The impulses that flow through the sympathetic nervous system are displayed in the iris like electrons shot onto the screen of a color TV. When these impulses are abnormal—i.e., when an organ malfunctions—the iris's fibers are thrown out of alignment. At the same time, chemicals and drugs present in the body are carried through the capillary circulation system and deposited in the surface layers of the iris as spots of discoloration.

This health-monitoring system, called the neuro-optic reflex, is probably the most exact and up-to-the-minute diagnostic tool doctors have for learning our total organic condition, capable of indicating up to three thousand disease conditions, inherited weaknesses, and the general status of the body.

By taking a photograph of the iris and placing over it a transparent grid showing which areas correspond to the body's various organs, iridologists can read spots, lines, and discolorations in the eyes for the body's general level of health; inherent constitutional strengths and weaknesses; nutritional and chemical needs; all stages of infections, inflammations, and toxemias; and the condition of the nervous system. According to the late Dr. Bernard Jensen, who pioneered the science of iridology in the United States and founded International Iridologists in Escondido, California, "[It] is not the last word in determining the diagnosis of the patient, but reveals inherent characteristics of the tissues in an organ. It shows tissue changes resulting from proper or improper treatment. It is a checkup on both the patient and the doctor as to whether the patient is improving."

Iridology can alert doctors to disorders of the heart, lungs, liver, and sinuses; to specific conditions such as a backed-up lymph system, a prolapsed colon, underactive glands, or an overactive sex drive; and to general conditions such as acidity, anemia, or arthritis. It can even locate an organ that has degenerated enough to be highly susceptible to cancer.

What's in an Iris?

Though iridology is a complex science requiring extensive training, there are basic checks we can make on our own and others' irises for quick analyses of general health.

First, make note of the irises' "constitution," indicated by the tightness and uniformity of the fibers. The healthiest physique is reflected in irises with the texture of fine silk, the fibers close and even. The more irregular and open-spaced these fibers are, the more weaknesses are present in the body's systems and organs. If the fibers are not only open but also especially light in color (in comparison to the iris's basic color), swollen, or inflamed, radiating outward from the pupil like rays from the sun, the body is being subjected to severe stresses that are taking their toll on the specific organs on whose iris-points these fibers lie. Acid build-up, pains, and discharges are all possible results of these stresses, and must be treated with not only rest but also more balanced nutrition.

Check also for bright red, orange, and yellow spots in the iris. These psori, or "psoric itch spots," represent inherited chemical deposits in the tissue corresponding to the spots' iris positions. If a white line surrounds a psora, there is irritation in that tissue. Tiny colored spots in the iris, known as toxin flecks, may be a sign of artificially introduced (rather than inherited) drug deposits in the body.

Holes, or lesions, in the iris indicate inherited or acquired weakness within the body. As with psori, the holes' positions indicate which organs are in this condition.

Radii solaris are long dark grooves that radiate outward from the pupil like the spokes of a wheel. They are the sign of a slow-moving, possibly toxic bowel, and indicate a need for inner cleansing and purification through diet.

Nerve rings, also called neurovascular cramp rings or contraction furrows, are formed by a buckling or pinching of the iris fibers, and appear as concentric circles in the iris. They warn that nervous stress is affecting the body's muscular system, which is storing this stress as harmful anxiety and tension.

At the iris's outer edge—the zone corresponding to the skin, hair, and nails—may be found a dark marking called a scurf ring or rim. It is the sign of an underactive, slowly eliminating skin in which toxic substances and metabolic wastes may be collecting.

Opposite in appearance to the dark scurf rim that may appear at the outer perimeter of the iris is the opaque white sodium ring, which has the appearance of the sclera (white) of the eye having crept up slightly over the cornea. In the past the sodium ring was most commonly associated with heavy exposure to salt, and could almost always be found in the eyes of seamen, salt miners, and the like. Today it is also referred to as a cholesterol ring, since it warns of excessive cholesterol and triglycerides as well. A person whose irises show this ring has difficulty metabolizing calcium, which settles in the joints along with inorganic salt compounds. Associated with this chemical imbalance are high blood pressure and hardening of the arteries—conditions that may be reversed, with the imbalance itself, through proper nutrition and modification of diet.

Just within the outermost zone discussed above is the zone corresponding to the body's lymphatic system. When lymphatic circulation becomes sluggish, congested with waste substances, small cloudlike spots resembling a rosary or a string of pearls will appear. The whitish color of this "lymphatic rosary" is a sign of inflammation resulting from this back-up; if the "beads" or "pearls" are light brown or yellowish, this condition has existed for a considerable period of time.

In general, an organ's health may be observed improving or declining as indicated by the color progression of markings in the iris. For example, in a blue eye an organ disorder begins as a white (acute) mark, then worsens to grayish yellow (subacute), gray (subchronic), and black (chronic). If treatment of the disorder is successful, the organ may be seen healing as the color process reverses, culminating in crisscrossing white healing, or calcium luteum, lines. These are the welcome sign that the body has generated new tissue both within the organ and, as a result of restored uniform nerve impulses, within the iris, sloughing off old cells and replacing them with new healing ones akin to scar tissue. Interestingly, when an organ is surgically removed, its corresponding iris reflex point freezes in its presurgical condition, never to register tissue change again.

Whether our pupils are revealing our heart's desire or our irises indicating an unhealthy heart, our eyes communicate nonstop information about who we are. It has taken modern science to prove that the eyes are not only the windows of the soul, but also the windows of the body.

8

EYE ADORNMENT

The Language of Beauty

If I could write the beauty of your eyes,
And in fresh numbers name all your graces,
The age to come would say, "This poet lies;
Such heavenly touches ne'er touched earthly faces."

—William Shakespeare, *Sonnets*

If you wish to love them, it shall be, by my faith, for their
beautiful eyes.

—Molière, *Les Précieuses Ridicules*

Early Eyepaint

Men and women first painted their eyes because they believed eye makeup possessed magical or religious powers. One example passed down to us from ancient times is the story of a painter who was going blind. In desperation he wrote to his son, "Bring me some honey for my eyes and some fat . . . and real eyepaint as soon as possible. . . . I want to have my eyes, and they're missing." Eyepaint, he believed, would restore his failing sight.

Soon people grew aware of the different effects they could achieve by applying certain colors to the eyes, and eye-painting became an art they used to enhance their beauty. Perhaps the earliest evidence of eye makeup being put to this use is from an ancient Sumerian tablet that describes Inanna, the goddess of love, as she carefully dresses herself. On her eyelids, we're told, she placed a colored ointment with a surprisingly modern name: "Let him come, let him come."

But it was the early Egyptians who began to develop eye-painting to an extraordinary degree, not for magical or religious reasons, but to protect themselves from the damaging glare of the African sun, to kill germs, and to repel flies and gnats. Narmer, the first pharaoh of whom we have record, was entombed with the slate palette on which he ground the malachite he brushed around his eyes. Though this green eyeshadow must have had quite a mystical effect, malachite (basic copper carbonite) was known primarily as an anitseptic. Other of Narmer's cosmetics contained hydrosilicate of copper, a preparation for skin damaged by the sun.

The uses of eye makeup soon grew beyond the purely protective. From Egyptian painting and sculpture and from implements and actual cosmetics found in the pharaohs' luxurious tombs, we know that the women of the time lavishly decorated their eyes—already their most dramatic feature—to achieve arresting effects. The brown-skinned Cleopatra was probably the most famous cosmetics user, though she was typical of the upper-class women of her time, whose methods of applying eye makeup were as sophisticated as ours are today. The Queen took great care to color her eyes in the finest detail, and even used special elbow cushions to steady her hand as she drew the delicate lines. She applied black galena (lead sulphide) on her upper eyelids, deep blue on the lids themselves, and bright green (malachite) on the lower lids. In her beauty box she kept containers of shadow powder, tubes of eye pencils, a bronze mixing dish, cosmetic pots, a polished bronze mirror with a carved handle, and bottles of colored ointments, some of them antiseptic.

Later in Egyptian history, galena was replaced by burnt almond shells, soot, or manganese dioxide, and malachite's green was duplicated by conifer resin. These cosmetics were prepared by grinding the main ingredients to a fine powder on a flat stone, then making a paste by mixing the powder with water or a water-soluble gum. The paste was applied to the eyelids with the index finger or with wood, bone, or ivory rods.

Perhaps the most famous of ancient Egyptian cosmetics is kohl, a mixture of powdered antimony and soot that was kept in special kohl-pots—clusters of four cylinders with long applicator brushes for darkening the upper and lower lids and thickening the lashes and brows. The famous black-eyed look is still used today by the Arabs, and was popularized in America by Theda Bara, the silent film actress of the twenties. The look recurred in the fifties, when actresses such as Elizabeth Taylor and Ava Gardner used a modern form of kohl to dramatize their eyes' dark beauty, striving for an Egyptian or Oriental effect.

For Beauty's Sake

Not that the application of eye makeup has always achieved its desired effect. The famous Jezebel, who married the Hebrew King Ahab, acquired a bad reputation not only because she worshipped Baal and drove the prophet Elijah into temporary exile, but also because she painted her eyes. When she heard that the rebel Jehu, who had killed her husband, was approaching the city, she "painted her eyes, and attired her head, and looked out at the window" (II Kings 9:30), hoping to seduce her enemy and save her life. But her efforts were to no avail. Jehu threw her out the window and a battalion of horses rode over her body until only "the skull, and the feet, and the palms of her hands" remained (II Kings 9:35).

The women of ancient Greece chose mulberry juice to make their dark eyes even darker, and from Greek painting and mosaic we know they achieved a lovely effect. But on hot days, according to Eubulus, an Athenian who wrote comic plays around 376 B.C., two purple rivulets flowed down their cheeks.

Pliny the Elder strongly disapproved of the Roman women's daily practices of painting their eyes with powdered antimony or ashes. "So ardent are they in the pursuit of beauty," he complained, "that they must even color their very eyes." But women were not Rome's only offenders. During the empire's most effeminate period, the court and patricians painted their eyes heavily. In *The History of the Decline and Fall of the Roman Empire*, Edward Gibbon tells us that the emperor Elagabulus, on first entering the Eternal City, appeared with his eyebrows darkened with antimony and his face painted red and white.

It *was* Rome's women, however, who in their ardent pursuit of beauty invented the most dangerous practices. As we mentioned in Chapter 7, they dropped belladonna ("beautiful lady"), a drug extracted from the roots, leaves, and berries of the deadly nightshade plant, into their eyes in order to dilate the pupils and make the eyes look larger, darker, and more glistening.

This practice continued in Italy through the 1800s, when some less courageous women took to moistening their eyebrows by rubbing them with a few drops of the less potent tincture of belladonna. These women still achieved that fascinating languorous look, but even this modified practice, when repeated frequently, led to impairment of vision and sometimes even blindness.

The use of other chemicals to change the eyes' appearance was equally dangerous. Some actresses and women of fashion made their eyes clearer and more sparkling by exposing them to prussic acid vapors. They placed a single drop of the dilute acid at the bottom of an eyeglass or eyecup, then held the glass or cup against their eye and threw back their head for a few seconds. During the Renaissance, some people even squirted lemon juice directly into their eyes to make them sparkle with tears.

Long eyelashes have always been reputed to increase sex appeal, since their fluttering or batting movements emphasize their owner's more alluring glances. Therefore it's not surprising that women have endeavored to lengthen their lashes by natural or artificial means. One now-obsolete practice they adopted to promote the length and silkiness of their lashes was "topping," or trimming the extreme tip of each lash. Beauty experts advised that this be done only occasionally, and that another person do the trimming to ensure the neatest possible job. Topping was most effective, these experts claimed, when begun in early childhood.

For today's woman who desires longer lashes, the style is simply to apply false ones, available for both the upper and lower lids, and in all lengths, colors, shapes, and degrees of fullness. Human behaviorists refer to these beauty accessories as supernormal aids, because they exaggerate both the movements of the lids and the natural length of one's own lashes.

Women have made their eyebrows more appealing by plucking or tweezing them into smoothly curving lines, stressing the difference between the male and female brows. Shakespeare had a special appreciation of "the right arched beauty of the brow," and of brows that were dark and fine:

> Black brows they say
> Become some women best, so that there be not
> Too much hair there, but in a semicircle
> Or a half-moon made with a pen.

As detailed in Chapter 2, a person's eyebrows have been thought to be one of the keys to his personality. If the brows have a high arch, sweeping upward from the nose to the lower forehead, they are said to signify a

Long eyelashes have always been reputed to increase sex appeal, since their movements emphasize their owner's more alluring glances. Mascara enhances the look.

dramatic nature, a person with style. Where did this belief originate? For years, actresses have plucked their
eyebrows into this dramatic form to make them more
distinctive-looking from the stage. It's not surprising
that people born with these brows should be thought to
possess all the talents and qualities of an actress: a sense
of timing, the ability to move easily from one role to another. Artificially shaped eyebrows of this type tell us
not only how their owner perceives herself, but also the
image she wants to project to others.

Eye-Catching

There have, of course, been other methods of drawing
attention to the eyes. At one time, European men and
women pasted small black circular patches resembling
beauty marks to their faces; eventually these patches
grew even more eye-catching as fancy shapes such as
stars and crescent moons became the rage. At the court
of Louis XV, the exact positioning of these decorative
patches took on subtle meaning. When a man or
woman wore a patch at the corner of the eye, it was interpreted as a sign of great sexual appetite.

To make their eyes look clear and brilliantly white
from the stage, actors and actresses began artfully applying eyeshadow and black eyeliner to sharpen the
contrast between the eyes and the rest of the face. To
give the illusion of larger eyes, they applied to the eyes'
inner corners a dot of white makeup, which when
viewed from a distance seemed to extend the white
area. These tinting and outlining techniques have been

borrowed by women in modern times, and, with modifications, are the basis of their makeup practices.

Actually, women were creating the bright, wide-eyed look long before the advent of sophisticated theatrical makeup techniques—as far back, in fact, as 1000 B.C. As we mentioned, in Cleopatra's day the trick was to outline the eyes with thick black kohl and slant them dramatically upward at the corners. This technique not only made the eyes look larger, but also gave the woman a certain air of alertness and intelligence.

Today, women create the large, bright-eyed look with a combination of techniques. Black mascara on the upper and lower lashes makes the eyes look especially brilliant, and some women accentuate the black by adding blue liner under the lower lashes. Dark eyeliner creates the definition between face and eyes for that alert, intelligent, focused look, and various shades of eyeshadow can give the eyes the same slanted appearance prized by the ancient Egyptians.

Makeup experts know that the eyeshadow colors that best enhance eye language are the natural tones such as beiges and pale golds, blues, and greens, since they softly complement the eyes—and their movements—rather than draw attention away from them. Keep in mind that the more attention you can draw to the eyes themselves, the better. Brightly artificial blues, greens, pinks, and purples in daring stripes that march to the brow are fine for the stage or for dramatic effect at a special party, but they do draw attention away from the eyes and can be disconcerting during a conversation.

Experts in makeup application know that the more they can high-light the eyes, the better. This woman has used iridescent eye-shadow to draw attention to her dramatically tweezed brows. Cleopatra achieved the exact same look.

Making a Spectacle

Today's high-fashion eyeglasses are another device for making the eyes look big and bright, placing in question Dorothy Parker's famous "Men seldom make passes at girls who wear glasses."

In reality, people have always taken advantage of the aesthetic effects they can achieve with eyeglasses. Members of the upper classes began wearing them—whether they needed them or not—because they imparted an intelligent, dignified appearance. Fad followed fad until glasses were little more than just another wardrobe accessory, to be worn regardless of the quality of one's vision. A popular variety consisted of two round lenses hinged through the handles and hung by a gold or silver chain around the neck, always handy for lifting and spreading like a V before the eyes. Later it became fashionable for a man to wear the single-lensed monocle wedged into one eye, while for a woman the lorgnette—a pair of eyeglasses with a long handle—was the ultimate refinement.

But people of a more practical nature dismissed the purely decorative eyeglasses as silly affectations. Johann Peter Eckermann perhaps expressed this attitude best when he wrote in *Conversations with Goethe:* "Wearing spectacles makes men conceited, because spectacles raise them to a degree of sensual perfection which is far above the power of their own nature."

Today, eye adornment in its various forms is a multibillion-dollar business—and one that will continue to thrive. For whether it's with eyeglasses, eye-lashes, or eyeshadow, people will always seek to drama-tize and enhance the most vital of the languages we speak—that of the eyes.

INDEX

Page numbers appear in italic for illustrations.

acid vapors, 161
adornment, eye, 157–68
  beauty marks and, 164
  eyebrows and, 162, 164
  eyelashes and, 161–62,
    163
  glasses and, 167
  history of, 157–62, 164
  makeup and, 164–66,
    166
Affect, Imagery, Consciousness
  (Tomkins), 4
affects, 4
Africa
  body's ability to reveal
    character and chief-
    tains in, 36
  Ethiopia, 123
  Kenya, 25
  Liberia, 127
  Sierra Leone, 25
  Tunisia, 120
Ahab, King, 160
Alexander, 36

Alfonso XIII (king of
  Spain), 121
Allport, Gordon W., 37
Amish, 129
animals
  eye contact and, 20
  eye-shape types and, 56,
    58–60
  personal distance and,
    110
  primate, 20, 22, 93
  staring and, 93–94, *94*
Antoinette, Marie, 51
appearance
  character and, 39–41
  of eyes, 33–34
  temperament and, 37
apple of one's eye, the, 141
approval-needs, 15, 16
Arabs, 26, 88, 159
Argus Panoptes, 129
Argyle, Michael, 13–14, 20
Aristotle (Greek
  philosopher), 35

Art of Seeing, The (Huxley), 107

Asia, 25, 26

See also Chinese; Mesopotamia; Orient

As You Like It (Shakespeare), 115

At the Back of the North Wind (Macdonald), 47

"Attitude and Pupil Size" (Hess), 144

autism, 20, 24

babies

bonding and, 20–21, *21*, 22, 23

whites of eyes and, 51

Babylonians, 149

Bacall, Lauren, 83, 84

Balfour, Clara Lucas, 115

Balinese, 12

Balzac, Honoré de, 39, 142

Bara, Theda, 83, 159

Bard College, 39

bars, 75–76

Bates, William H., 105, 107

beauty. *See* adornment, eye

beauty marks, 164

bedroom eyes, 53, 82–83

belladonna, 148, 161

Berlin (Germany), 37

Birdwhistell, Ray, 2–3, 4

blindness

as barrier, 30

belladonna and, 161

irises and, 150

night, 150

staring and, 88

blinking

as cut-off, 103–5

eye seduction and, 77, 79

gaze behavior and, 11

meanings of, 5

body mannerisms, 6

bonding, parent/child, 20–21, *21*, 22, 23

Bororo Indians, 25

Bow, Clara, 83

Boyer, Charles, 83

brain

color of eyes and, 43

emotions and the, 4

mental functions and the, *38*

pupil size and the, 140

Brazil, 126

Brontës (English novelists), 39

Browning, Elizabeth Barrett, 46

bumps of the head, 37, *38*

business

face-readers for hiring in, 40–41

social distance in, 133–34

staring and, 95

videophones in, 27

Byron, Lord, 73, 120

Canada, 2–3

Casanova, 142

Cervantes, Miguel de, 69

Chapman, George, 9
Chattanooga Institute of
    Human Studies, 43
Chaucer, Geoffrey, 39
Chin dynasty, 36
Chinese
    eye shapes as animals by,
        56
    face reading by, 36
    glitter of the eye and, 53
    irises link to body health
        by, 149
    pupil size and, 142
Churchill, Sir Winston, 34
civil inattention, 96
Cleopatra (Queen of Egypt),
    158–59, 165, 166
closed eyes
    as eye cut-off, 105–9, *106,*
        108
    meanings of, 5
College of Physicians and
    Surgeons (Columbia
    University), 51–52
color, of eyes
    animals and, 93, *94*
    iris colors, 42–49
    linked to behavior and
        personality, 41
Columbia University, 39, 51
Conan Doyle, Sir Arthur, 39
concave eye, 60, 61
Conduct of Life, The
    (Emerson), 9, 87
conjunctiva, 149
contraction furrows, 154

Conversations with Goethe
    (Eckermann), 167
convex eye, 60
Crawford, Joan, 62
cultural variations, 25–26,
    99
cut-offs, eye, 101–14
    blinking and, 103–5
    closing eyes and, 105–9,
        106, 108
    common, 111–14, *113*
    equilibrium and, 101–3,
        114
    mental illness and, 109–11
    personal distance and,
        110–11
cutting, 95
Cyclopes (giants), 129

Darwin, Charles, 2, 17
day in the life of eyes, 6–7
death, 51
depressives, 23, 109–10
Deuteronomy, 139
de Verre, Aubrey Thomas,
    46
Dickens, Charles, 39
distance, personal, 110–11,
    133, 135
domination, eye, 130–38
    in daily lives, 132
    dominate-subordinate
        gaze of, 130–32, *131,*
        133, 134
    eye cut-offs as opposite of,
        114

domination, eye (*cont.*)
  manipulation and,
    134–37, *135*
  salesmen and, 134,
    136–37
  social distance and,
    133–34
  See also evil eye; eye-threats
Don Quixote (Cervantes), 69
dragon eyes, 59–60
DuBarry, Madame, 83

ears, 35
Eastern Pennsylvania
    Psychiatric Institute, 3
Eckermann, Johann Peter,
    167
eeshon, 142
Egyptians, 116–17, 158–59
Eibl-Eibesfeldt, Irenäus,
    11–12
Einstein, Albert, 34
Ekman, Paul, 4–5, 18–19
Elagabulus (emperor),
    160–61
elephant eyes, 59
Eliezer, Rabbi, 117
Emerson, Ralph Waldo, 7–8,
    9, 87
emotions and eye behavior,
    2, 4, 5
England, 97
envious eye, 119–22
equilibrium, 101–3, 114
Essays in Physiognomy
    (Lavater), 36–37

Ethiopia, 123
Eubulus (Athenian author),
    160
Europe
  color of irises and, 43
  evil eye and, 117, 128
  gaze behavior and, 26
  history of physiognomy
    and, 36
  phrenology and, 37
Evasive Eye, 111–12, 114
Evening in Greece (Moore),
    48
evil eye, 115–29
  in death, 129
  envy and, 119–22
  history of, 115–19, *118*
  methods of combatting
    the, 122–29, *124, 127*
  See also domination, eye
Exline, Ralph, 13, 14, 17
*Expressions of the Emotions in
    Man and Animals, The*, 2
eyebiting, 117
eyebrows, 62–67
  eye adornment and,
    162–63, 164, 166
  eyebrow-flash, 11–12
  history of physiognomy
    and, 35, 37
  kinesics and, 3
  man-made, 62
  moles and, 62
  reading, 63
  remedies for defects of, 40
  shapes of, 63–67, *66*

signals involving, 5–6
"Eye Color: A Personality
    Guide" (Phillips), 43
eye contact
    approval-needs and, 16
    autism and, 20
    cheating/lying and, 17–19
    etiquette, 25
    gaze behavior and, 10, 13
    between parent and child,
        20, *21*, 22
    public speakers and, 29
    schizophrenia and, 20
    shyness and, 19–20
    women vs. men and,
        14–15
eyeflash, 11
eyeglasses
    as adornment, 167
    as gaze barrier, 28–29
    gestures and, 6
    See also sunglasses
eye-insults, 95–96
eyelashes
    eye adornment and,
        161–62, *163*
    eye seduction and, 77–78
    physiognomy and, 53–55
    remedies for defects of,
        40
eyelids, 3, 53–55
eye management, 96, 97–98
eye-painting, 157–59
eye pick-up, 69–71, 75
eye power, 12
eye profiles, 60–61

eye punctuation, 11
eye roll, 52
eye-shape types, 55–60, *57*
eye-threats, 91–93, *92*, 130,
    131, 134

face-reading, 39–41
Facial Affect Scoring
    Technique (FAST),
    4–5
fascinatio, 125
fascinum, 125
feige, 125, 126
Félise (Swinburne), 45
Ferdinand, Archduke, 51
fish eyes, 59
flight distance, 110–11
France, 99
Frank, Anne, 34
French, 12, 83
Freud, Sigmund, 78
Friesen, Wallace, 4
Fugito, Stephen S., 16
full-stop glance, 12

Gardner, Ava, 159
Gary, A. L., 43
gaze behavior
    aversion, 10, 24–25,
        111–12, *113*
    barriers and, 26–30, *31*
    bonding and, 20–23
    cultural variations of,
        25–26
    dominant-subordinate,
        130, 132–33, 134

gaze behavior (*cont.*)
  eye tests, 31–32
  glitter and, 53
  leering, 14
  mutual-gaze games, 20
  patterns of, 13
  primates and, 20
  rules of, 10–16, 23–26
  sheep's eyes, 14
  temper and, 16
gender, 14–15, 75–79
Geneviève, Saint, 88
Gentleman Usher, The
    (Chapman), 9
Gestalten, 39
Gibbon, Edward, 160
glance(s)
  body, 71–72
  eye seduction and, 79–81,
    80
  full-stop, 12
  language, 10
  sidelong, *84*
  terminal, 12
glasses. *See* eyeglasses; sun-
    glasses
glitter, 53
Glover, John, 43
Godiva, Lady, 88
Goebbels, Joseph, 34
Goethe, Johann Wolfgang
    von, 37
Goffman, Erving, 30, 87,
    96
Gone With the Wind, 77
Greeks

  combatting evil eye and,
    123
  envious eye and, 119
  eye adornment of, 160
  eye shapes as animals by,
    56
  irises link to body health
    by, 149
Guatemala, 121
Guitry, Lucien, 83

Hall, Edward T., 133
hands, and the eyes, 6
Han dynasty, 36
Hebrews, 142
Henried, Paul, 83
Herder, Johann Gottfried
    von, 37
Hesiod (Greek poet), 82
Hess, Eckhard, 140, 143–45,
    146, 148
Heywood, Thomas, 82
Hidden Dimension, The
    (Hall), 133
Hippocrates (Greek physi-
    cian), 35
*History of the Decline and Fall
    of the Roman Empire, The*
    (Gibbon), 160
Hitler, Adolf, 51
hog eyes, 59
horned hand (mano
    cornuta), 125
horse eyes, 58
Huxley, Aldous, 107
hypnosis, 51–52

identity, eyes and, 7
Inanna (goddess of love), 158
India
  envious eye and, 120
  gaze patterns in, 26
  methods of combatting evil eye and, 123, 126
Indians, 2–3, 25
  See also Native Americans
Indus Valley, 149
International Iridologists, 153
iridology, 151–53
irises
  health and, 149–56
  Liljequist and, 151
  personality and color of, 43–50
  physiognomy and, 42–50
  pupils and lightness of, 146–47, *147*
  size of, 42
  von Peczely and, 150–51
  See also iridology
Italy, 121, 148, 161

Japanese, 23, 50, 126
Jensen, Bernard, 153
Jesus, 117
jettatore, 121
Jewish weddings, 128
Jews, 126
Jezebel, 160
Jung, Carl, 78

Kassem, General Abdul Karim, 51
kaynahorah, 126
kayn ayn ha'rah, 126
Kennedy, John F., 51
Kenya, 25
kinemes, 3
kines, 3
kinesics, 2–3
Kings II (Book of Bible), 160
kohl, 159, 165
Kutenai Indians, 2–3

Lake, Veronica, 79
Landon, Letitia, 49
Langley Porter Neuropsychiatric Institute, 18
Language of the Body, The (Lowen), 23
Latin America, 24–25, 26, 72, 125
Lavater, Johann Kaspar, 36–37
leering, 14
Les Précieuses Ridicules (Molière), 157
les yeux en coulisse, 83, *84*
Liberia, 127
Liljequist, Nils, 151
Lincoln, Abraham, 51
lion eyes, 56–57
Longfellow, Henry Wadsworth, 44, 47
long-looking, 73, *74*, 99

look-and-away technique, 98
lorgnette, 167
Louis XV, King, 164
love, eyes and, 69–85, *84*
    eye pick-up and, 69–71, 75
    glances and, 71–72,
        79–81, *80*
    long-looking and, 71–74
    male eyes vs. female eyes
        and, 75–79
    See also sexuality
love motive, 16
Love's Mistress (Heywood),
    82
Lowen, Alexander, 23
Luo man (of Kenya), 25
lying, 17–19
lymphatic rosary, 155–56

Macdonald, George, 47
Machiavellianism, 17–18
macrobiotics, 51
Maidenhood (Longfellow), 44
makeup, 164–66, *166*
    See also adornment, eye
mal occhio, 121
Man and People (Ortega y
    Gasset), 83
manipulative eye, 134–38,
    135
mano cornuta (horned
    hand), 125
Manwatching (Morris), 111
Masque of Pandora, The
    (Longfellow), 47
Matthew, Book of, 83

Mencius, 139
Mende people, 25
mental illness, 23–24,
    109–10
    See also schizophrenia
Mesopotamia, 149
Mexico, 121
microsleep, 104
Middle East, 123
Midsummer-Night's Dream, A
    (Shakespeare), 45
Mitchum, Robert, 83
moles, 61–62
Molière, Jean-Baptiste
    Poquelin, 157
Mona Lisa, 34
monkey eyes, 58
monocles, 167
Monroe, Marilyn, 51
Moore, Thomas, 48
moral looking time, 91, 98
Morris, Desmond, 111
Moses, 35–36
mutual-gaze games, 20
My Kate (Browning), 46

Napoleon III (French
    emperor), 120–21
Narmer (pharaoh), 158
Native Americans, 124, 149
    See also Indians
Navaho children, 25
Near East, 125
need-affiliation, 16
nerve rings, 154
neurooptic reflex, 152

neurotics, 23
neurovascular cramp rings, 154
New York City, 40, 97
Ngo Dinh Diem, 51
Nizam's Daughter, The (Landon), 49
Nyoiti, Sakurazawa, 50–51

ocular bonding, *21*
Oedipus, 78
Orient, 43, 128
See also Asia
Origin of the Species, The (Darwin), 2
Orpheus, 87
Ortega y Gasset, José, 83
Othello (Shakespeare), 72
Ovid (Roman poet), 82

Pakistan, 26
palming, 105–6
Papuans, 12
Parker, Dorothy, 167
paseo, 72
peek-a-boo hairdoo, 79
Peeping Tom, 88
Pennsylvania, 129
Perfumed Garden, The, 88
personology, 41
Phillips, Michael, 43
phrenology, 37, *38*
Physiognomica (Aristotle), 35
physiognomy, 33–67
    of eyebrows, 62–67, *66*
    of eyelashes, 53–55

of eyelids, 53–55
eye profile and, 60–61
of eye types, 55–60
of glitter, 53
history of, 34–39
lines around the eyes and, 61–62
moles and, 61, 62
physical appearance and, 33–34
state of the art, 39–41
of whites of eyes, 50–52
See also irises
"Physiognomy" (Saunders), 37
Physiognomy (Wolff), 39
Picture of Dorian Gray, The (Wilde), 33
Pius IX, Pope, 121
plane eye, 60, 61
Pliny the Elder (Roman scholar), 160
Points on the Map of the Face, 36
Polt, James M., 144–45
primates
    eye-threats and, 93
    visual bonding and, 20, 22
    whites of eyes and, 10
    See also animals
privacy, 96–97
Prometheus Unbound (Shelley), 33, 82
Proverbs, Book of, 117
proxemics, 133
psori, 154

Psyche (de Verre), 46
Psychology of Interpersonal Behavior, The (Argyle), 13–14
Psychology of Marriage, The (Balzac), 142
pupa, 142
pupilla, 142
pupillometrics, 143–44
pupil size, changes in
    definition of pupils and, 139–40
    emotions and, 140–41
    experiments on, 143–46, 148
    factors that cause, 140
    history of observations about, 141–42, 148
    irises and, 146–47, *147*
    patterns of, 141
    sexual arousal and, 142, 145, 148–49

Rab (Hebrew scholar), 117
radii solaris, 154
Reich, Wilhelm, 23
Roberts, John, 119
Romans, 160, 161
Romeo and Juliet (Shakespeare), 44, 72

salesmen, manipulative eye and, 134, 136–37
Salluste du Bartas, Guillaume de, 83
sanpaku, 50, 51, 58

Saunders, John, 37
schizophrenia
    cut-offs and, 110–11
    eye contact and, 20
    staring and, 99
Science Digest, 43
Scientific American, 144
sclerology, 149
scurf ring, 155
seduction, eye language of. *See* love, eyes and
sexuality
    bedroom eyes and, 53–54
    eye adornment and, 164
    eyebrows and, 6, 64, 65
    eyelashes and, 161–62, 163
    eyelids and, 54–55
    eyes as symbols and, 78–79
    pupils and, 142, 145, 148–49
    skin lines around the eyes and, 62
    See also love, eyes and
Shakespeare, William
    from As You Like It, 115
    on eyebrows, 64, 162
    from *Midsummer-Night's Dream, A*, 45
    from Othello, 72
    from *Romeo and Juliet*, 44, 72
    from Sonnets of, 116, 157
    from *Venus and Adonis*, 49
sheep eyes, 58

sheep's eyes, 14, 73
Sheldon, W. H., 41
Shelley, Percy Bysshe, 33, 82
Shifty Eye, 112, 114
shyness
    Evasive Eye and, 112
    eye contact and, 19–20, 73
    language of love and,
        72–73
Shyness (Zimbardo), 19
Sierra Leone, 25
Signoret, Simone, 83
skin lines, around the eyes,
    61–62
sleep, 102–3, 104
snake eyes, 59
social distance, 110–11, 133,
    135, *135*
Socrates (Greek
    philosopher), 36
sodium ring, 155
Sodom and Gomorrah, 87
Sophocles (Greek
    playwright), 78–79
South America, 25
Spain, 37
speakers, public, 29
Speigel, Herbert, 51–52
Stammering Eye, 112
staring, 87–100
    as acceptable, 89–91
    animals and, 93–94
    business communications
        and, 95
    cross-cultural differences
        of, 99

domination and, 95
eye-insults and, 95–96
eye-threats and, 91–93, *92*
history of physiognomy
    and, 35
meanings of, 5
polite eyes and, 96–98
as rudeness, 88–89
stories about, 87–88
Stigma (Goffman), 30
Studies in Human Commu-
    nication project, 3
Stuttering Eye, 112, 114
sunglasses
    blinking and, 79
    as gaze barrier, 27–28,
        31–32
    See also eyeglasses
Swanson, Gloria, 83
Swinburne, Charles, 45

Talmud, 35–36
Taylor, Elizabeth, 159
telephones, 15, 26–27, 30
television newscasters, 29–30
Tennyson, Alfred, Lord, 88
terminal glance, 12
That the Eye Bewrayeth
    (Wyatt), 69
Tomkins, Silvan, 4
toxin flecks, 154
Tunisia, 120

University of California in
    Riverside, 16
University of Colorado, 25

Valentino, Rudolph, 83
Venus and Adonis
    (Shakespeare), 49
Vernon, P. E., 37
vertical eye. *See* plane eye
videophones, 26–27
von Peczely, Ignatz, 150–51

Watson, O. Michael, 25–26
West, Mae, 83, 84
whites, of eyes
    four-white-sided, 59
    physiognomy and, 50–52
    primates and, 10
    three-white-sided, 58
widened eyes, meanings of,
    5
Wilde, Oscar, 33
winking

eye seduction and, 78
history of physiognomy
    and, 35
meanings of, 5
witches, 117
Witches' Hammerer, The
    (Malleus Maleficarum),
    117
Wituto Indians, 25
wolf eyes, 58
Wolff, Werner, 37, 39
Wyatt, Sir Thomas, 69

Yin-Yang, 51
You Are All Sanpaku (Nyoiti),
    50

Zimbardo, Philip, 19

ABOUT THE AUTHOR

Evan Marshall heads his own literary agency. A former book editor and packager, he has contributed articles on writing and publishing to numerous magazines and is the author of *The Marshall Plan for Novel Writing, The Marshall Plan Workbook,* and *The Marshall Plan for Getting Your Novel Published.* He is also the author of the popular Jane Stuart and Winky mystery series. He lives and works in Pine Brook, New Jersey.